Singled Out

Singled Out

A Civilized Guide to
Sex and Sensibility for the
Suddenly Single Man–
or Woman

Richard Schickel

The Viking Press/New York

Copyright © 1980, 1981 by Gideon Productions, Inc.
All rights reserved
First published in 1981 by The Viking Press
625 Madison Avenue, New York, N.Y. 10022
Published simultaneously in Canada by
Penguin Books Canada Limited

LIBRARY OF CONGRESS CATALOGING IN PUBLICATION DATA
Schickel, Richard.
Singled out.
1. Single men—Psychology. 2. Single men—Sexual
behavior. 3. Interpersonal relations. 4. Dating
(Social customs)—United States. I. Title.
HQ800.3.S33   306.7   80-54080
ISBN 0-670-64710-1

This book is based on the article "The Great Second Chance," which appeared originally in *Esquire* magazine.

Grateful acknowledgment is made to the following for permission to reprint copyrighted material:

Chappell Music Company: Portions of lyrics from "At Long Last Love" by Cole Porter. Copyright © 1937 and 1938 by Chappell & Co., Inc., owner of publication and allied rights. International copyright secured. All rights reserved.

Charles Scribner's Sons: Excerpt from "Winter Dreams" in *All the Sad Young Men* by F. Scott Fitzgerald. Copyright 1922 by Frances Scott Fitzgerald Lanahan; renewal copyright 1950.

Printed in the United States of America
Set in CRT DeVinne

To D.
Ever,
R.

Introduction:
The Ad Hoc Life

Whatever it says out there on the jacket, I wouldn't want anyone to think that this is a guidebook in any conventional sense of the term. It is not based on the latest scientific findings, unless you regard one man's attempt to digest and analyze and even quantify a little bit his own extensive, if erratic, experiences in this field as a scientific enterprise. Nor is it a survey, unless my talking to all my friends of recent years about most of the matters discussed herein counts as a survey.

As a matter of fact, for a long time I didn't know what exactly it was that I was writing—except, like all the things that have given me pleasure of late, it was the result of a lucky accident. It worked like this: a couple of years ago I got to be friends with a chap named Jerry Goodman, who, when he's not being "Adam Smith" is a/k/a George Jerome Goodman, whose idea of a part-time job is to be one of the executive editors of *Esquire*. We fell into the habit of dining together at various swell spots around town to talk about this and that. (In a different kind of book that sort of behavior is known as "male bonding," and, especially if you're a single guy, it is essential to your sanity.) Anyway, Jerry, who is married and lives in Princeton, took a particular delight in listening to my tales of the woes and wonders of living free, and being literary gents of the journalistic and critical persuasion, we used to make all sorts of sociological and psychological generalizations based on the flimsy evidence of my experience and overheards. Finally one day Jerry suggested that I could probably write a piece for his magazine about what it was like to suddenly turn single after you've been terribly married for about fifteen years.

It seemed like a good idea at the time, and in a trice it was done. (A trice, by the way, is a period of not less than three months of relentless preoccupation with a subject, and no fun at all.) In due course *Esquire* published the results, and I couldn't have been more surprised by what happened next. In something over a quarter of a century of writing nothing I've done—no book, no article, no TV show—has ever elicited the response that that piece did. Letters, phone calls, even people stopping me on the street. And the responses were overwhelmingly favorable.

By which I mean that the piece seemed to have some sort of consoling effect on people. They were pleased to discover that the sorts of things that had been happening to them had been happening to someone else—same problems, same anxieties, same crazinesses. Nothing can be more pleasing to a writer. Or, as it happened, more inspiring. People kept suggesting new areas to explore, giving me anecdotes and ideas about the material I had already published. On top of which, I found that the damned article wouldn't let me alone. I kept having second and third thoughts about what I'd written, wanting both to expand and refine the thing. One more trice and that, too, was done.

I still don't know exactly what category or genre this slender volume belongs to, though in my mind it has come to seem more of an autobiographical essay than anything else. I know that here and there it is a little more prescriptive than autobiography ideally should be, and it is certainly less formal in tone than that sort of writing usually is. But what I was striving for, stylistically, was something like the sound of those conversations with Jerry with which the project started: colloquial-literate, I guess—I hope—you'd call it. Anyway, it is as true a rendering of a five-year experience as I can make it.

But, obviously, anyone's experience has its limits. I mean, if you're looking for advice on the etiquette of singles bars, forget it; I've never cruised one. My dear chap, there are limits! Similarly, I've never tied up a girl or played in a trio or gone to Sandstone—or even to a massage parlor. You'll have to speak to Gay Talese about all that.

In short, I can only write from my own perspective, which is that of a 47-year-old, middle-class, middle-brow American male, who once had a reasonably good marriage that, in time, turned into a reasonably bad one. From which, anxiously— not to say terrified—I exited, full of misinformation—not to say dark fantasies—regarding the unknown world that this book is about. If I had an audience in mind as I wrote, it is the me of five years ago, rather more of an innocent than a man of my age and alleged sophistication should have been. Looking back, I wish that there had been something like this to read at the time. Or maybe just someone who had acquired the experience I've since acquired and was willing to talk about it, frankly and simply, as I've tried to here. I might have avoided some mistakes. Or not. But I sure would have felt less like an explorer halfway up some fast-running creek without a paddle.

The fact that this book is autobiographical, that a lot of its concrete details are drawn from my own life, should not, I think, deter anyone from using it profitably. If the response to that little *Esquire* piece—only about a fifth as long as this—is any indication, the particulars of my case do not in any way prevent the intelligent reader from sensing the commonality of the situations I've found myself in. Or the universality of the emotions underlying them. Indeed, the most surprising thing about the response to the article was the fact that far more women than men took the trouble to write and say they knew exactly what I was talking about. I figure if a 32-year-old female junior executive in Grand Rapids, Michigan, can feel such a strong sense of identity with an Old Crock writer who's lived by his wits in New York for a quarter of a century, I must have stumbled on something—an attitude as well as a subject—that is not exactly exotic.

About that, one last point. As I developed my original essay into this book, a new thought—new to me, anyway—began to take form and then to nag at me. That is, that all of us, no matter what age, sex, marital status, or station in life, are, nowadays, living *ad hoc* lives in a chance universe, a place where you really can't count on anything anymore. It seems to me that the suddenly single—those who were once part of a family they fondly believed to be an immutable verity until they discovered that it was as mutable as yesterday's political poll—have particular reason to understand this existential point. And, that it is not necessarily to be construed as an argument for hedonism—or against it, for that matter. All I want to stress is that we who have been "singled out" (see, that title was not lightly chosen!) have a particular obligation to conduct ourselves with a certain grace and gallantry, even, if you will, as examples to those who still cling to the illusion that life is a fixed and stable process. Knowing what we've come to know, we surely are bound to behave toward one another with a certain kindness, civility, and tact, to ease one another's passage through this changeable and occasionally brutal world with consideration and gentleness—just plain common decency, not to put too fine a point on it. Finally, this book is written in aid of that cause.

Singled Out

Tragic Victim of Divorce

Maybe you've recently lived the scene. Maybe you're pretty sure you're about to live it. Surely you've imagined it, things being what they are today. Anyway, its outer aspects (but not, I think, its rich, full-bodied inner dynamics) have been captured in movies like *Starting Over* and *Kramer vs. Kramer,* various television shows, novels, nonfiction psychobabble, and God-knows-what-else our wondrous and amazing culture may have recently churned up. It goes like this: you've just shut the door on what the lawyers will shortly take to calling "the marital residence." You're standing there, a suitcase in each hand, looking a little like Willy Loman about to explore the New England territory. In this moment of awful finality you're still too stunned to be grateful for the fact that you will no longer have to hear about her need for "more space" or listen to invidious comparisons between her growth rate and yours in matters spiritual, psychological, intellectual, and sexual. (How could you not have realized that all those years you were living with a courtesan *manquée*?) All you feel is shut out and sorry for yourself, terribly, terribly sorry for yourself.

There's a sense of loss, of course, of life's game plan being busted. There is also, let's face it, just the slightest sense of being unmanned, especially if—as it was with me—you are over 40 and familiar with the traditions of divorce which, until recently, held that it was the male's prerogative to break things up, to find a fresh face with whom to share his midlife crisis. Women have only recently seized this option for themselves, and men have yet to create a set of folkways, wisdom, and just plain camaraderie comparable to that which women have built up out of decades of bitter experience. Most males have very little to fall back on to ease this awkward passage. Filling the mind whenever it idles, there are the small anxieties: Why didn't you learn to cook something besides a steak? Where do you go to get a good price on lamps? And, towering above such mundane concerns are the ones that usually begin with the phrase, "I just can't imagine ..."

"Just can't imagine asking a girl for a date." "Just can't imagine actually making a pass at someone." "Just can't imagine waking up in a strange bed." Whatever. This is understandable. It has, after all, been years since you actually went out on dates, or had actually to woo a lady, charm her to bed. Oh, maybe you got drunk with somebody at the Pig Iron Convention a couple of years ago and went back to her room, but you know that doesn't really count. And that most civilizing and educational of institutions, the long-running extramarital affair, has never really taken hold in America; you're not among the lucky minority (one-third of all married males, the statisticians tell us) who have actually experienced that invaluable exercise in the upkeep of romantic skills.

Indeed, standing there, buttoning your topcoat against the chill, you can't help remembering that you really weren't much good at all that stuff the last time it was legal for you, when you were single in your twenties. You were always kind of all thumbs, weren't you? Either too blunt or too shy, maybe even a little sneaky. (You remember: the arm draped casually over the back of the lady's seat at the movies, the comradely pat on the shoulder, all those accidental-on-purpose brushings and touchings. Boring! And as un—if not counter—productive now as they were then.) Besides which, you gather from the papers, nowadays women are, since liberation, more critical, more demanding than they ever were. And you've just had your fill of *that*.

Hopeless, just hopeless, you say to yourself, trudging off in search of a cab. Oh well, maybe there's something on television. Now wait a minute. You know, and I know, there isn't. What I know, and you don't, is that things aren't as bad as they seem, that the only thing you have to fear is, yes, fear itself. In other words, what this book represents is a collection of folk wisdom, which has only been acquired after a heap of livin' by the author, and by trusted colleagues of both sexes, in the several years since I was the guy standing there on the sidewalk, burdened by a lot more than my suitcases.

A More Realistic Assessment

The first thing to do is remind yourself that you are no longer a 24-year-old idiot. You have probably acquired over the years since you were a certain amount of wit and wisdom which, though lost on your sometime spouse, may very well prove interesting, even entertaining, to an intelligent stranger of the opposite sex. (And if she's not intelligent, what are you doing with her anyway?) We are also assuming here that you have not screwed up your entire life, that you've done at least reasonably well in your work, which means that you've acquired along the way a certain amount of influence, maybe even power. This, too, has its charms for women—though it is generally not aphrodisiac to flaunt it too blatantly. Finally, you now have something else you didn't have when you were starting out, namely some disposable income, not all of which The Plaintiff, as she may come to be known in certain circles, is going to take away from you. Indeed, one of the advantages of the new style of separating—where the woman leaves the man, or anyway insists he take a walk—is that psychologically it reverses things. It used to be that the male, the leaver, got the guilt while the female, the leavee, suffered a certain ego loss. But if she asks you to leave, that equation turns around. Now she gets the guilt and, consequently, the bad bargaining position when you settle down to settle up. No one expects the injured party to pay for the privilege, and it is all right, gentlemen, to act a little more woebegone than you actually feel while you, she, and the lawyers are striking the deal. With any luck you should come out with enough to stay out of Ronald MacDonald's clutches—on the first date, anyway.

But I digress. The basic point to remember is that during the years that have intervened since you last went out on a date, you have ceased to be a nobody and have become a somebody, and that's very reassuring to women. It means, of course, that you can take them nice places, which cheers everybody up, but more important, your date doesn't have to engage in the desperate game that preoccupied her counterparts when we were all kids and she couldn't tell, any more than you could, how you were going to turn out. Since nobody likes to hook up with a loser, the fear that you, that anybody, might turn out to be one has always tended, understandably, to make women cautious of young guys. Derive, therefore, both pleasure and confidence from your substantiality. You might even want to paste up near your telephone the inspiring words of a young woman who responded to my dithering during those first dreadful days of separation, when my romantic imagination had completely failed me. How airily she informed me: "Oh, you've got nothing to worry about—you're single, solvent, and straight!" And how right she was! It remains the best assessment of the competition I've ever heard.

If you stop to think about it, you are in what Stendhal—in *Love*, the only great work of nonfiction that I know on this subject—described as an ideal condition. To wit: "A prerequisite of love is that a man's face, at first sight, should reveal something to be respected and something to be pitied."

Self-Image

But, you say, status has not been achieved without a certain cost. Your hairline has gone north; your waistline, despite the racquetball, has gone east and west. No denying it—you're just not the really cute guy you once were. Don't worry too much about that—unless you've entirely grossed out, in which case you ought to do something about yourself just on general aesthetic principles. Physical perfection simply doesn't mean as much to women as it does to men. This excellent quality results from the fact that they do not have our long and dismal tradition of objectifying the opposite sex. Charm, wit, and style actually count more with them than, say, a neat pair of pects, as a glance around any first-class restaurant will tell you. Look at all those splendid creatures dining with guys old enough to be their fathers. (The American female's endless search for her absent Daddy is another factor in your favor, but that's a dark realm not to be lightly entered upon, so I won't.)

One caution, otherwise known as Poor Richard's Theorem: Achievement will get you laid, but it won't get you loved. That is to say, it will grant you the privilege of initial access, but nothing that can be described as a permanent relationship. At first, the delights of putting the theorem into action will be enough for you, but there will come a time when the brief and the casual will not satisfy, when you will press someone for something more solid and be rudely awakened by the discovery that status, social appropriateness, mutual interests, all that jazz often don't mean a thing when a lady comes right down to making a permanent choice. It happened to me recently, and she chose one of life's losers, a permanent failure who, besides, treated her with truly strumifying indifference. Go figure. But be prepared.

Perhaps, though, we're getting a little ahead of ourselves here. Weren't you the guy we last saw standing around on a corner with your suitcases in hand? With a really nasty wind rising behind you?

Getting Busy

Remember those old aviation movies in which, as soon as someone crashed (but was lucky enough to walk away from it), the squadron commander made him take another plane up? Immediately. No shilly-shallying. The idea was that the only way to conquer fear was to confront it quickly and boldly, not to let it fester in the dark. Well, gentlemen, what can I tell you? Knot that flowing silk scarf dashingly at your throat, pull down those goggles, and—how shall I say?—contact!

I know. I know. You've got a million things to do. Alphabetize your half of the LPs. Hit the thrift shops looking for just the right moose head to hang over your new fireplace. Buy circus tickets so you don't have to talk too much to the kids on your first "visitation." (Yes, I know that's what ghosts do to haunted houses. And the metaphor is going to seem painfully apt for a while. Moreover, since the cure for continuing to think of the old marital residence as home-sweet-home, the wellspring of your territorial imperative, is to stake out new turf, you're correct to get right at all that fussing and fixing. Do not, I pray you, linger long in that first sublet or, God help you, at the transient hotel, living out of a suitcase.)

But first things first. Make a date. Make it before you move out. Make it, if you can, for the first night you're on your own. And without any grandiose hopes or dreams. Just pick out a nice lady, somebody you think it would be pleasant to have dinner with. And then have dinner with her. Pleasantly. Period. You're not ready for anything else. You need merely to dabble your toe in these new waters, paddle around a bit in the shallow end. Stay on this side of the ropes. No running. No diving. No larking about. Besides, to pretend to be ready for anything more would be grossly unfair to the lady. You will be, in time, and if she has a nice evening with you, she'll very likely be willing to bide her time for a few weeks until you're ready for something a little more *sportif*.

Yes, you do too know who to call. She's the new lawyer down the hall who smiled so prettily when you asked for the paperwork in the Continental Fidelity matter, even though she was pretty sure it had already gone to Central Files and was going to be a bitch to find. She's Herb's secretary over at Acme Nut & Bolt—the one who slips you onto his calendar even though you didn't call three days in advance for an appointment. She's Ms. Blodgett, your opposite number at Dorkodyne International, who stayed until nine that one night in order to expedite your shipment of half-spanners so the line could keep running the next morning—and laughed so gamely at your desperate jokes. Her name, in short, is legion. She is all the pleasant, unruffled, smiley-voiced women you haven't dared let yourself think about these past two or three years while you and Marion were "trying to work things out." If she's going steady or living with someone, she'll tell you quite directly that she has other preoccupations—no offense taken. If not, she probably doesn't have anything better to do next Sunday than try out that new Thai restaurant with you.

So brace up, spruce up, and, having attended very closely to the next section, prepare to have a surprisingly good time.

The Birds Is Coming

A lady of my acquaintance said recently: "I want to fly with an eagle, but I keep ending up with parakeets." Now, she means many things by that metaphor, but it should be noted that the salient characteristic of parakeets is that they talk too damned much. It is not considered good form to go on and on about the late unpleasantness at home. To be sure, many women will politely inquire about it, cannily hoping to gain some insight into your character thereby—which is precisely why you should clam up. For let's face it, it was probably not your finest hour, and until you've fully digested the experience, the early aftermath isn't either. So the thing is, bring a little shaping art to bear on your tale. At best it may work as an O'Hara short story; if they want to read Sidney Sheldon let them go out and buy a copy. The well-told anecdote, the lightest touch of rue, the manly admission of a few faults of your own—above all, an air of gallantry about the whole thing—these comprise the ticket. Think of the brave lads who fought the Battle of Britain, all chin-chin, chow-chow, and stiff upper lip. And don't just think of them; do an impersonation. But no horror stories.

In due course you will encounter female parakeets, and after you've stayed up until four a.m. a few nights in a row, listening to their woeful stories of cruelty and injustice, you, too, will come to appreciate the virtues of brevity in this matter. Unhappy former families are all alike, and even the people who advertise for companionship in the personals column of *The New York Review of Books* often specifically state that they're not interested in hearing from the recently separated. No sad songs for them. They may be desperate, but they're not *that* desperate.

Tuning In

As your third-grade teacher used to say, "You can't learn anything if you're talking." But you can't talk if you're listening. So shut up, at least for a while. Among other things, what you're embarked upon at the moment is one of life's great learning experiences. So there is no better time to start cultivating the lost art of flapping your ears. You'll be surprised at the pleasures it offers.

I know what you're going to say. You're going to say that you're a world-class listener, an immortal in the field. We all think we are, just as we all think we are, at heart, great romantics—though common sense should tell us that if even a tiny percentage of the population that considers themselves beyond instruction in either matter actually were, then there would not be so many of us in the pretty pickle that this book is about.

But let's not argue the point. In the interest of saving time, I'm willing to stipulate that there hasn't been a listener like you since Freud. But remember, you've been traveling in what Freud's followers—vulgar fellows—like to call a dyad, or in plain English, a pair, for years. And it's a funny thing, but people don't really confide in couples, even if one member happens to be absent for the moment. I don't know why this should be so. Maybe it's because they instinctively understand that there's no such thing as confidentiality when people are cohabiting on a permanent basis—pillow talk, you know. What I do know for certain is that when you are singled out, one of the first and most impressive things you're going to discover is what a huge, varied, and, indeed, lunatic life has been going on out there while you were going to PTA meetings. Secret drinkers! Abusive and/or neglectful husbands! Promiscuous wives! Discreet affairs! Indiscreet affairs! At least one of these will turn out to have been between two of your friends, and you never suspected a thing!

Such doings! A regular Peyton Place you've been living in. And nobody told you nothing. Well, they will now. And it's going to help you put what's going on in your life into, shall we say, a somewhat wider perspective, which at the very least will prove hugely entertaining. At best, it will prove highly instructive. Not just because you will discover that the comings and goings of the single life, the sudden changes in your emotional climate (in love—or what seems to be—one day; out of love—or what seems to be—the next) are a commonplace occurrence in your new set. Though that, in itself, can be terribly consoling, since compared to the stability of married life—even if it is an unhappy and even illusory stability—the ups and downs of your new life are bound to bring on a certain occasional queasiness.

No, I'm thinking of something a little more profound when I speak of this new perspective you're going to gain. Not to toot our own horns too loudly, but I have come to believe that single people, especially those who have been married and have endured the trauma of watching their share of that institution break down, are in touch with the most basic fact of life in our times. Namely, how transitory everything is. How you can't—and shouldn't—count on the permanency of anything. I've come to believe that this is a blessed state. It gives urgency and pungency to experiences that a false sense of stability can never impart to them.

I mean, if you are certain, for example, that a love affair is forever, then you are going to labor under the delusion that there is no hurry about sampling all its joys, that there is no need to tell your partner how lovely she looks this morning, or how sweet you find it that she bothers to put a fresh flower on your night table every evening. If, on the other hand, you know that anything can end at any time, that what is here today may very well be gone tomorrow, then maybe you'll be wise enough to experience whatever that anything is as fully as you can, while you can. Maybe you'll even be wise enough to rededicate yourself constantly to whatever it is you care about—your love, your work, your children, your stamp collection, if that's where some small part of your heart lies. By so doing, you may actually, paradoxically, achieve something that is pretty close to permanent. Or as close as anyone is going to get to it these days, anyway.

But whether or not this sense that life is pretty much one long improvisation leads to a new level of thoughtfulness, it is going to make radical changes in the cast of supporting players in your life. For it is going to direct you more and more toward people who share your new turn of mind, separating you from your old friends of the married years, which is going to hurt a bit. It's not merely that they no longer have much in common with you, or that you have less to learn from one another, given your new situation. It's that, after the first flurry of obligatory dinner invitations, at which they are given to making policy statements about how they feel that both of you were friends and that they don't intend to make a choice between you and The Plaintiff—"Oh, go ahead, choose," I always wanted to say—you are going to make one of two interesting discoveries about your relationship with dyads past. The first, and more likely, is that they are going to seem just a trifle smug and boring to you. Some of them *are* going to want to hang over the back fence of your life and hear your war stories, but most of them are going to look at you rather oddly after you've told a few, even if they asked to hear them in the first place. I kept getting the feeling that I'd told a dirty joke in the wrong company on those occasions.

And those are the people whose marriages are actually ticking over rather smoothly. Far worse are the evenings with couples who are experiencing a certain dyadic strain. To them—especially as you cease to be a figure of woe, start taking on more raffish lineaments—you are going to be perceived as a rather threatening presence: someone who has undergone the experience that taunts and tempts the unhappily joined and has lived to tell the tale. To a marriage that's feeling peckish, you're about as welcome as Typhoid Mary. In time, of course, quite a few of those marriages will sunder, and it may be at that point that you can renew one or more old acquaintances from it. In the meantime, you might care to keep at hand this quotation that I've kept around my desk for some time. It appeared, anonymously so far as I know, in *Le Monde* some years ago: "The sickness of the family is the fear of risk. Its credo is the economy of self, out of which comes the prohibition of all intense emotional activity."

There's a lot of truth in that, and it explains why, for the moment, you're going to have a surprising number of chilly—anyway, awkward—evenings with a surprising number of your old friends. And why, just naturally, you're going to find yourself gravitating more and more toward people who are, like yourself, at emotional risk, engaging in those messy and intense encounters that distinguish the early stages of single life. In the stories they are going to tell you you are going to find, aside from the sheer pleasure of the tale, the lore of your new subculture, the cautionary wisdom you will require as guide and comfort for the months ahead.

The Transitional Woman

Yeah, but you gotta talk to somebody. Bless your heart, of course you do. That's why God invented the Transitional Woman. More than likely you already know her—somebody down at the office, maybe the lady down the block or over at the tennis courts. (If, right after you separate, she starts asking you to fill out her doubles game, then you know she has it in mind to help you out during this difficult time.) The main thing about her, however, is that she's somebody you already feel comfortable, possibly even confidential, with. In fact, if you're honest with yourself, you'll admit that she's been drifting quietly through your fantasy life over the years—especially since she got *her* divorce a couple of years ago. Anyway, she's been where you now are, seems to have learned the ropes, and to have survived. And is, above all, simpatico. You will derive much emotional profit from pouring out your troubled heart to her. Besides which, it's not scary to ask her for a date or even into your bed. You *know* her. She's nice. She's not going to laugh at you or otherwise put you down.

Swell. Have fun. But watch it! Statistics tell us that the majority of second marriages are between people who knew each other before their first marriages broke up, which says a great deal, I think, about just how chicken-hearted we all are.

We're scared of rejection and scared of being alone, and therefore in a mad rush to cure both conditions. If you are of that cowardly stripe, then you need read no further. The transition you're going to make with the Transitional Woman is going to be right back into marriage. I am against this on principle. I think your second marriage, and mine (or maybe I should say our second "arrangement"), is going to be better if you've really sampled the pleasures and perils of freedom, not to mention the infinite variety of womanhood that is presently available to the interested man. If nothing else, you will be grateful for the calm of domesticity when it finally arrives. Best of all, you will feel that the lady you decide to share it with really is someone you chose out of this great wide, wonderful world.

This does not mean that Transitional Women are bad people. Actually they are terrific people by and large, and as the years go by you may very well find yourself looking back ruefully on the accident of timing that brought her into your life before you were ready for her. On the whole, though, the true function of the Transitional Woman is the restoration of your self-esteem, helping you to put the past behind you by making you realize that you actually have a future in the realm of human relations.

I want to emphasize that I am not speaking cynically. I'm not kidding when I say that if only you had met your transitional lady later, and as a stranger, the chances are that you might marry her, since she's so nice and all. Experience—mine, that is—merely teaches that for no reasons beyond a perfectly natural restlessness and curiosity, you're probably going to want to move on after a few healing months. When you do, treat her kindly (as she did you). And don't worry—you'll get your chance to redeem your debt because, just as sure as you're born, some lady is going to make you into her Transitional Man, and break your heart at the end of that process. You will, of course, always remember to send a Christmas card to your TW—and maybe take a sentimental turn with her on the dance floor at her wedding. Transitional Women, being also rather traditional women, nearly always have a proper wedding—even if it is their second time around.

Beyond the Transitional Woman

Or, Where Do I Go from You? It is entirely unfair and completely superficial to place women—anyone—in categories. It is offensive. It fails to take into account the infinite variety of humankind. There, liberal piety having been satisfied, we can proceed to what seem to be perfectly obvious generalizations about the kinds of people you'll be running into out there.

Career Women. Now listen, this is important. I have discovered only one inviolable rule, which is: never get involved with anyone who is not working. And I mean seriously working—ditsy little part-time jobs in art galleries don't count. What you want is a woman who is serious about her career, absorbed in it. It is true, of course, that we are developing a breed of women who, like too many men, have no room in their lives for anything but their careers, and like those men they can be terrible bores on the subject and pretty damned perfunctory about everything else, including sex. But they are still a minority. And, at that, they are generally preferable to women who sit around collecting their alimony checks and burnishing their sense of injustice. There is no room in their gloomy self-absorption for you, or anyone. And the whining will make you crazy. Women who are really trying in their work are, perforce, involved in something larger than themselves (except, of course, actresses, who are to be avoided at all costs). To put it simply, they are alive in the world and thus make for awfully good company. I have read complaints from males that such women are overly competitive, and I suppose a few of them are—just like us. But mostly I've found this not to be so, and that a fringe benefit is that they are just naturally more understanding of our professional problems than women whose only business dealings are with the butcher.

Feminists. It is extremely important to understand that this term is not a synonym for career women. As a matter of fact, I think it is neither synonym for nor description of any woman you are likely to encounter anywhere in the real world.

This information may come as a surprise to you if all you know about the subject is what you hear on the talk shows or read in the papers or gathered from The Plaintiff when she was borrowing from feminist ideology in order to buttress her arguments against you. I'm sure that women who would describe themselves, first and foremost, as Feminists do exist in small numbers. In New York, for instance, they seem to specialize in giving seminars on the feminist theory of filmmaking, or novel-writing, or basket-weaving, all of which are duly reported in the *Village Voice* and the *SoHo News.* Also, they seem to spend a lot of time giving and taking karate lessons. But, as I say, you are not likely to encounter many of them in normal society. And if you do, you are not likely to pass much time with them. You are not, are you, going to drift up to a woman at a cocktail party and engage her in conversation if you have not read in her manner certain welcoming signs—a pleasant laugh, for example, or a ready smile as she listens to someone's monologue? That grim one standing there bristling in her blue jeans—she's giving you fair warning, at least, and you'll be well-advised to heed it. She's not interested in what you're peddling. So unless unreasonable challenges unreasonably excite you, why don't you take that suspicious scowl at face value?

I do not wish to imply by the foregoing that women in our time are unaffected by the feminist carry-on of recent years. Of course that nice lady you invite to join you for a hamburger after the party believes in the Equal Rights Amendment. Who doesn't? Of course she is wary of men who are looking for a combination cook-housekeeper and stepmother to their children. She should be. It may be that her response to certain troubles down at the office will have a bitterness about it that will surprise you. Why not? Women, after all, are underpaid, compared to men, in the working world, and are indeed subject to certain harassments and indignities that we do not suffer. When these matters arise in her conversation, it is not ideology you are listening to but simple descriptions of the reality she has discovered in her daily rounds, simple questions about the inevitability of that reality that she is more than entitled to ask.

But it cannot be emphasized too strongly: the mass entrance of women into the competitive arena has not turned them into ball-busters. On the contrary, I think you'll find that women who are serious about their careers are more practically sympathetic, more intelligently responsive to whatever professional problems you happen to bring home than ladies whose experience of the working world is limited to that year they spent as a publishing house reader between college and marriage, and who don't really understand the rules of the game in which you're playing. On the whole, feminism, as the New Woman understands and practices it, has, paradoxically, made her more feminine. If by "feminine" you mean a person who can bring those two highly developed female capacities, feelings and intuition, to bear on a competitive world they now know a great deal more about than they did a decade or two ago.

Married Women. There's just one rule here: have affairs only with those who are happily joined in wedlock—with someone you don't know. I know it sounds as if there's some inner contradiction in that statement, but the fact is that many marriages are quite all right, friendly and companionable, with but one thing lacking—lively sex. If you can provide that and not be a nuisance about wanting to be more deeply involved, you will both have a swell time, and you'll have the added satisfaction of feeling that you're doing your bit to keep the divorce statistics down, supplying the one element that is missing in her otherwise contented life. My longest-standing relationship—well over three years in duration—was of this character, and I must say that, until a year ago, whenever I considered making some sort of permanent connection elsewhere, the thought of giving up those sweet afternoons with my married friend was a factor in cooling things off. Then, of course, things changed. But we'll get to that later.

As for women whose marriages are not happy, stay away. All they do is bring their complaints about their husbands into your bed, and the bitching and moaning drowns out all the fun. For example, a friend of mine recently got involved with a woman whose spouse, at her endless urging, had presented her with a Mercedes. When she was finally about to take possession, my friend looked forward, at the least, to a change of subject, but no, the husband—wretched man!—had found a dealer out of town who offered him a considerable discount; the next time she turned up she was complaining that the cheap bastard had made her take a 300-mile round trip over the weekend in order to accept delivery. And so on and on it went, through the watch that wasn't quite the model she wanted, the couch that was either too large or too small (I forget which). Finally, as well you might imagine, the litany of complaint drove my pal out of that particular game. As well it should have. Obviously there are unspoken complaints that drive any married woman out of her legal bed. Let them remain unspoken!

Live-in Ladies. Nowadays, of course, you will encounter lots of women who are living with men "out of wedlock," as we used to say, and the same basic rule that applies to the formally united applies to them, too, since, manifestly, many of them are going to turn out to be as bored with their sex lives as anyone who has been legally married for a few years. Indeed, with women like this you must proceed with special caution, for there are a couple of wrinkles in the situation that could trip you up with a particular lack of grace.

You see, staying together *sans* certification requires a much greater act of will than staying in a marriage does. The presence of children and a normal, healthy dread of the divorce ritual substitute for will in a marriage, encouraging the search for discreet alternatives to the irreparable breach. Not so for the lady who is only *morally* committed to a relationship. Theoretically free to walk out any day, she must, each day, consciously rededicate herself to the thing. The result is that her freedom is far more apparent than it is real. Which means that you're likely to encounter a lot more guilt with one of them than you are with a married woman, strange as that may seem. So your liaison is going to be attended by glooms and fidgets that are, ultimately, deep downers. Also, the fact that she is technically free may encourage you to press her for more of her time, and more of a relationship, then she can actually give you. This leads to general crossness and fights.

Another point about the technically free: they are, as a class, the last stronghold of the great American tradition of cock-teasing. Not since you were working sorority row in the fifties are you likely to have encountered anything quite like it. Not long ago I was encouraged to take one such woman out for what turned out to be a very pleasant dinner. When I took her home her roommate was briefly absent, and I was invited to help her walk her dog in the canyon behind her home. (This was out west, and, oh, by the way, ladies with dogs, especially little yappy ones, are to be approached with great self-protective circumspection.) Anyway, much delicious kissing and grabbing ensued out there amongst the sagebrush and the rattlers. After I returned to New York I got a letter from her: "Next time you're in town, drop over and I'll show you my succulents." (She has a cactus garden, but she is no stranger to metaphor.) Well, you know what happened: I returned, all lathered up, and for my pains got to pick up another check and to listen to a philosophical disquisition on the joys of permanent relationships. ("Everything just gets better and better.") She devoutly hoped I would soon find such stability.

This was not the first time something like that had happened to me. You see, these ladies have the same need we all have to gather reassurances that we remain attractive. But for them that need is all too easily gratified. French-kissing in a Chinese restaurant, the quick grope in a discreetly parked car, rubbing longingly up against you on the corner of 53rd and Fifth, a few glasses of wine under the belt to provide an excuse next morning—all true autobiographical incidents—do the trick. Why proceed messily further, they think, when you have, either by initiating or responding to a sexual overture, already answered the essential question? One understands, is even sympathetic. But it is also a pain in the ass.

The Ages of Women. In casting about for suitable partners we must consider not only professional and marital status but also, alas, age. Now there are nice women available in every age group, but I've found that for a man in his forties, women passing through the odd-numbered decades are likely to prove most satisfactory.

I know lots of guys my age like women—actually, I think of them as girls—in their twenties, but that's the easy way out:

acting the mentor's role, or feeling like a hell of a fellow just because you can keep up with a kid. My trouble is that I can never figure out how to sustain a conversation with them, since their frame of cultural reference and mine don't coincide at all. The younger ones are actually a little bit vague about Clark Gable, and, predictably, their eyes glaze over with an honest emotional puzzlement if you play them a cut or two of Willie Nelson's "Stardust." Those golden oldies really don't mean a thing to them. Conversely, they are full of innocent discoveries; one recently asked me if I had heard of Evelyn Waugh, assuring me he was a marvelous writer I'd really like. Very sweet and all that, but not the basis for even a modest-sized relationship.

As for women in their forties, it seems to me that many of them have been ill-used by recent history. Some, naturally, are what might be termed classically desperate—left in the lurch by straying husbands (see *supra*) or, on the other side of the coin, looking up too late from their careers and finding that all those years of living alone have set them too rigidly in their ways to be really cheerful lovers. But the ones who present the hardest (and sometimes saddest) cases for the approaching male are those who have been betrayed by feminist ideology. They have actually fallen for a kind of party line, left their marriages in favor of some late-blooming career (see *supra* again) and are now in the process of discovering that their new lives are no more fulfilling than their former ones. Or that even if they are fulfilling on one level, life has many levels.

As a result, one encounters among women of this age a pervasive, if often unspoken, sense of disappointment, a feeling that perhaps they were born too soon, that various rights and privileges that younger women seem able to grasp easily as their natural due come hard and awkward to their older sisters, and anyway turn out not to be as nifty as they were cracked up to be. All this tends to make many women in their forties edgy emotionally and stiffish sexually, full of dos and don'ts put forth querulously. You get the impression either that it's your job to turn sex into a total reparation for the bad deal they've had or that there is nothing you can do, in bed or out of it, to redress their grievances. Neither position is, shall we say, a gratifying one.

The thirties, on the other hand, are a very good time. They are for everybody, as you doubtless know from your own experience. It's a time when you're beginning to sense your own potential and to realize it. Also, it's the only decade we have when some of us, anyway, function more or less as grown-ups yet are untouched by that plague of all the years to come, a sense of one's own mortality. But for women these days it is, or should be, truly a golden age. They are the beneficiaries of two revolutions: the (decently) feminist and the sexual. The former allows them to pursue their professions without undue guilt, either about letting their ambitions hang out or about delaying (or entirely forgetting about) getting married and having children. As for that other revolution—well, they have these needs, see? And they go about the business of satisfying them in a nicely straightforward fashion. Oh, it's a good idea to keep some candles on hand because they are not insensitive to the traditional pleasantries; they do like to bathe the bedroom in a nice romantic glow, for example. And don't forget the soft music, either. But you should remember items like that no matter who you're seeing, klutz. All I'm stressing is that by and large you can ask them a direct question and get a direct response, no arm wrestling on the couch, no moral debates, plenty of oral sex. If you haven't been around much lately you're going to discover, among the thirty to forty crowd, what it is not too much to call a new breed of woman.

You're also going to discover—if you're very, very good, and very, very lucky—another new breed: new to you, anyway. That is, the woman of a certain age. Now, as we get older that "certain age" advances, too. Which means we are talking about women in their late forties and early fifties. The majority of them are merely continuing their forties by other means, that is to say, in a mood of increasing frenzy. (I've known one or two to revert completely, and grotesquely, to the kittenish style of their teens.) But there is this tiny, inspiring minority who have actually lived and learned. What profound pleasures they offer! You see, every conceivable line, on every conceivable subject, has been tried on them, and most of them have this permanently arched eyebrow which got that way by looking askance at all the ploys you think you might try on them. But they are wise, tolerant, patient, and usually very funny. You can't do anything with them but state your business honestly and take seriously whatever response they offer. Sexually they have learned what you haven't—you poor, dumb, horny bastard—namely, that you can get along without it if you have to. Therefore, they tend to be sweetly choosy. But if they decide you might just possibly pass muster (and they're not talking athleticism, they're talking civility), they are warm and affectionate, not wildly demanding or crazily possessive either.

Best of all, they understand that just because you've had a nice time in bed this is not a sign that marriage or other permanencies must immediately be considered. They tend to think that way because they've come to really treasure their independence. Or, as one of them wrote to me recently: "I luxuriate in my ability to be alone, to choose my own hours, pace, and pleasure. Many women come to this, I suppose, or dream of it, having gone through the discipline of bringing up children. I have it—forever, if I choose—and so I've become unattractively selfish, with no wish to submerge myself in another person and his happiness. . . ." I guess I'd take out that "unattractively," but you see what I mean. This is the liberation beyond liberation. Besides which, being (obviously) old-fashioned girls, they have a pleasant way of getting up with you in the morning to fix you a nice cup of properly brewed coffee—no instant—and offer a little cheerful conversation before sending you on your way.

Michael Caine as Role Model

All right, there are all these terrific women out there, and you've had fair warning about the types that aren't so terrific. Now what? Well, the first thing is to underwhelm them. Even if you've been living in Saudi Arabia the last decade, you will have heard the lip-curling contempt with which women pronounce the word *macho*. They mean it. And let it be stipulated, here and now and forever, that the attitudes they are summarizing in that bit of shorthand really *are* boring and vulgar, and unless you make your living as a nose guard in the NFL, you're going to have a hell of a time acting out the role with any degree of realism anyway. I have discovered, over the course of much pillow talk in recent years, that the movie star many mature middle-class American women quietly like best is Michael Caine, and the thing they like best about him is his vulnerability, which is blended with good humor, pleasant manners, and a generally sweet disposition. By the end of the picture he may have bedded more women than Clint Eastwood ever does, while equaling his body counts in the action sequences; but out there in the audience it's Caine who often seems more cuddlesome.

So don't think Clint or Burt Reynolds when you take the lady home. Even Burt and Clint aren't imitating Burt and

Clint anymore—not full time, anyway. More and more Clint is limbering up those adorable dimples of his in nice, goofy comedies that allow his natural sweetness and good humor to shine through. As for Burt, when he is not cheerfully parodying his old *machismo* manner, he is often to be found—as in *Starting Over*—doing a very passable Michael Caine impression. No dummy, he. And no feeb, either. In these roles he's just a nice guy who isn't afraid to admit to the odd doubt, the sudden fear—and he holds his strength in reserve, not invisible, but never flaunted or wasted. In short, he's human, and not afraid to show it.

Foreplay– and Foul

By the preceding I don't mean to imply that women like indecisiveness or, worse, little-boy routines, where you kind of scuff your toe in the dirt and try to aw-shucks her into bed. That used to work for Jimmy Stewart and that crowd, but not anymore it doesn't. By the time you get her home, and she's invited you in for a drink (it is, of course, the same promising signal it has always been), she will have sent you plenty of clues as to what her interests are—the hand that brushes yours more than is strictly necessary to make her conversational points at dinner, the touch of a knee, or her true, eye-sparkling delight when she discovers that you, too, liked *The Right Stuff* or *Manhattan* or *Barry Lyndon* or whatever your cultural touchstones are—these are things to which attention must be paid. And the very act of paying attention, of really concentrating on her, considering the number of egomaniacs running around loose these days, should stand you in good stead. When you get home and are having that drink, what you should do is simply display some physical affection, firm but gentle (no ripping at the lady's blouse, please), followed by a direct question, politely put. A modicum of discussion may follow, but if it crosses the line to tedium, I think a quick but not sulky exit is in order.

However, we have arrived here at the first tricky bit in the seduction ritual. You have got to evaluate her initial turndown carefully. It may be an invitation in disguise. Anyway, it is subject to several interpretations. The first is that she would like to be swept away on what she can think of next morning as a tide of irresistible passion. ("I don't know what I was thinking of.") If that's the case, you're just going to have to make a delicate judgment about what are her true interests, and be prepared to misjudge and be misjudged (and feel like an idiot), but persist—unbuttoning buttons, unzipping zippers, maybe seizing her bodily and propelling her firmly in the direction of the bedroom. The silliest incident of this kind in my files involved a blind date, who willingly accompanied me to my place after dinner, necking and grabbing as we drove there, then came all over funny when we started to get down to serious business on the couch. Talking a blue streak, fumbling at this and that clothes fastener, I hustled her toward the stairs that led to the bedroom. She resisted but didn't resist, if you know what I mean. "Please take me home, I really can't stay, it's late," she kept saying, but her little legs kept climbing. Her last "I really must go" was uttered as she lifted her adorable bottom up off the bed, the better to facilitate removal of her underpants. She proved to be an enjoyable bedmate, but if you want to know the truth, I thought the whole episode was really stupid, and degrading for both of us. As I say, this was an extreme case, and usually resistance, assuming everything else is pleasant between you, is *pro forma*, a bow to the strictures of yesteryear, the girl her mother fondly believed she was raising—and did; it's just that customs change.

On the other hand, there is a second interpretation to her refusal. That is, that she just doesn't want to. Tonight. There are still people in this world who like to think things over, and they often turn out to be very good people indeed. It is not written that just because there's a sexual revolution going on out there, everybody has to get laid on the first date, or even the second. (After that, well, you'd better reevaluate the whole situation.) Thus, a strategic withdrawal may be indicated—and all the more reason not to extend the conversation unduly or to leave in a huff. Do not, under any circumstances, fall into what I've come to think of as The Trembling Arab Syndrome. This is a condition first identified by a woman friend of mine who travels in international circles and has a rather sweet vagueness about her. Anyway, she recently inquired whether I'd ever been in a position where I was forced to turn down an Arab. Before I could protest, she added, with that quick perception for which she is locally famous, "No, I don't suppose you ever have. Gosh, it's awful. They get terribly quiet, and then they start to shake all over."

You take my point, I hope. You are both theoretically adults. If she doesn't want to, she doesn't want to. So be a good sport about it, for God's sake.

Which advice extends to the third, and most dismal, possibility in all this, namely, that you just plain don't turn her on. This is very likely to have a bad effect on your morale and to make you cranky. That's human, but there's no reason to make a big fuss about it. I know you've just suffered the biggest putdown of all from The Plaintiff, and each new one is bound to hurt rather more than it would in different circumstances. But the fact is that no one—probably not even Warren Beatty—is going to score every time he gets the ball. So, don't sulk. Don't take it personally. If you're going to play in this league, you've got to learn to play with the little hurts.

The Heart of the Matter

Let us not, however, dwell unduly on what can go wrong. Let us imagine that through the magical combination of common sense and enthusiasm, you have actually made it to the bedroom. You are now faced with a lovely array of possibilities that you don't want to think about too much lest they either overwhelm you or disappear in the mist, like Brigadoon. And if you think you're going to get a lot of specific, practical advice here, forget it. I mean, I don't know if you should tickle her ear with your tongue. Some people like that sort of thing and some don't, and you'll just have to learn, slowly, to trust your impulses.

There are, however, a few fairly obvious matters that I feel obliged to get out in the open right here. Probably the first among those issues you have to face up to is what has come to be known as performance anxiety. You've been reading a lot about that lately, mostly in the form of complaints from our fellows as reported to the sex surveyors. What's happened, of course, is that women are getting around more than they used to, in the course of which they are discovering guys who really know how to turn them on, and working off this wider base of comparison, they are beginning to expect more of their subsequent gentlemen callers. You see any reason why they shouldn't?

The first thing to do about this state of affairs is to accept it—as a challenge. I mean, it's a given in the life of our enlightened times, so there's no point in getting crabby about it. And besides, knowledge is, as they say, a two-way street. Some of those ladies, thanks to your predecessors, will have picked up a pleasant trick or two to surprise and delight you. And then, stop to think a minute: as a physical act, sex requires somewhat less coordination than serving a tennis ball or whapping the ball solidly down the fairway with a No. 3 wood. There's nothing really to worry about on that level. Finally, don't worry so goddamn much about failure. I don't care what the other guys claim in the locker room; there isn't a man on earth who hasn't, at various times, failed either to get it up or keep it up. It's another of the little hurts ("Welcome to the NFL") that we've got to play with. But one of the very substantial fringe benefits of dealing with more experienced women is that this is one of the experiences they've all had. I've never met one who wasn't terribly understanding and sympathetic about it when you flop. You're tired. You're preoccupied. You're trying too hard. Whatever. You might also bear in mind that neither your tongue nor your fingers are subject to temporary malfunctions, so it is not necessary to deprive your friend of her pleasures just because you've pooped out for the moment. And, in the way of those things, the act of pleasuring her may very well inspire you, and so forth and so on.

There is, however, one thing about which your modern woman is not the least bit understanding or sympathetic, and that is sexual self-absorption on the part of the male. It is something you're going to hear about across a dozen pillows in the months ahead. One well-traveled lady of my acquaintance once did a little imitation of the typical American man's idea of dynamite foreplay. "First, he twiddles you here for about thirty seconds," she said, touching one of her nipples, "then he sort of distractedly massages around down here for another minute or so," she added, touching her pubic triangle, "then he sticks a finger in to see if you're ready. Then he climbs on."

Blunt talk. But I've heard the same story, less vividly put, enough times to believe she speaks truly. I honestly don't understand what's going on (actually *not* going on) out across this broad land of ours. At the risk of sounding sentimental, I just want to say that, to me, a woman's body is one of the miracles of creation, and that the most miraculous thing about being invited into a woman's bed is that she is permitting you voyage—to touch, to taste, to look, to smell. To know, in short.

It seems to me that the kind of physical contact I'm talking about here is, in some sense, the equivalent of conversation, the function of which—between a man and a woman who are strangers—is to discover what pleases, what displeases one another, to find out what each of them has in common with the other, and also what they have to teach each other. The poet Louise Bogan put it very well: "I like lovemaking when it is well-informed." What we are talking about here is a form of grace and civility, of *politesse* if you will, and that implies a serious, thoughtful, humorous, and tender interchange, the leisurely technique of which, if it does not come naturally to you, requires more sober concentration to practice than any of the exotic positions you're going to find in the illustrated sex manuals that are the pillow books of our culture.

Concentration! It is as basic to sensual pleasure as it is to good writing, for example, or, to employ the more widely understood sporting metaphor, catching or hitting a ball. I know an actor, a strange-looking little man, balding and bug-eyed, whose specialty is playing weirdos. Except for the strangeness of his countenance, you wouldn't pay him the slightest heed. But women do, and while those Harry Hotcombs who play the leads in the TV shows in which he gets guest-star billing are standing around adoring themselves, this character is making off with all their leading ladies. "When you look like me," he says simply, "you have to try harder." By which he means that he gives his most earnest attention to whatever the lady is saying or asking, concentrating all his energies on someone who very shortly begins to believe she is the most fascinating creature in the world. If a certain amount of bedazzled testimony is to be believed, his conversational manner carries over into the bedroom, and it is a lesson to us all. Pay attention, dummy!

It is, I must say, depressing to feel that the foregoing paragraph was necessary, and I know that to some of you it is going to sound like a lot of fuss and bother, perhaps not worth the effort, especially since it has become so easy, of late, just to lurch from one-night stand to one-night stand, the illusion of intimacy easily encouraged, not to mention the feeling that you're a hell of a fellow. For you, I think, it's probably necessary to point out that there is a nice, neat, cheering bottom line to all this. It's best summarized by a fragment of an old song lyric: "I give to you, and you give to me ..." In other words there are certain things you'd really like to have happen, sexually, but which are not all that easy just to up and ask for. Well, if you're giving, nicely and gently, guess what's going to happen? Somebody is going to give back in the same spirit. This is called nonverbal communication, and there is a sweet effortlessness to it that will touch your heart and maybe one day just change your life as well.

An Afterword on Afterward

"How come every beautiful woman I know thinks she ought to lose ten pounds?" I asked a friend of mine the other day. "I don't know," she replied. "How come every man I go to bed with wants me to tell him he's the best lover I ever had?"

Let's just stipulate it: We're all insecure, we all have these nagging questions about ourselves, our attractiveness, our desirability. And there is not a bedroom you're likely to enter that doesn't have its population of ghosts, not a woman you're likely to encounter who hasn't employed her sex's unique capacity to fake orgiastic pleasure. Knowing that, why do you feel compelled to ask such a stupid question? I mean, really! It's admitting that you're in need of ego support and that you're not too bright to begin with. Sex is not the U.P. Writers' Football Poll—not in most women's heads anyway—and you're not going to be assigned a ranking. They grade—the better class of ladies, anyway—on a pass-fail system, which is operational over the entire semester you are together and takes into account many matters other than performance in bed.

Women are not raised the way we are, with the win-lose metaphor central to the way we look at the world and determine our place in it. Or, to put it simply, sex may be play to a woman, but it's not a game in the sense that scores are kept and standings compiled. Therefore, a single performance in bed, or even a short series of them, is not likely to determine how you rank in her league. Of course, you have your pride, and you never can tell—so you'll want to do your best and leave her with a nice memory, in case this turns out to be just one of those (brief) things. Anyway, you should have a desire to make a good impression on someone you feel warmly enough about to have come this far with. If, on the other hand, it turns out that this is the beginning of something serious, you'll discover that the competition with the ghosts is not going to be won or lost in the course of one encounter on this playing field.

As for your occasional suspicion that she might be faking it, well, lucky her and lucky you. Lucky her, because don't you wish sometimes you could just sort of lie back and supply the appropriate sound effects? Lucky you, because really women *are* more complicated physiologically (and maybe emotionally) when you come right down to orgasm, and the odd bit of deception they practice now and again should be looked on as a gift, a way of saying "thank you" if your attentions have been honorable. And also a way of saying "Do call again when madam is home."

So bite your tongue. Don't pop that question. If you're doing well sexually you'll know without asking—you'll feel it in yourself and she'll be telling you in all sorts of subtle, and not so subtle, but entirely delightful, ways. If it's not so hot between you, you'll know that, too, without asking. If that remains the case, over several evenings, I advise disengagement. You may be a better man than I am, and therefore capable of participating in dialogues intended to improve your mutual performance, but I think they're a total drag, an attempt to substitute will for magic, and, in their final effect, congealing rather than liberating.

Okay, I'm just a romantic fool, but I think love is an art, not a science, which means that it is, among other things, a happy accident, impossible to force into being. I know, I know, you have to work at it, same as you have to work at a book, spend time and energy on it; but the good stuff, in books and in love, just seems to bubble up out of the unconscious. In my time, I've been the best lover in the world, and I've been the worst—same guy, same style, same enthusiasm, and sometimes with the same woman. I think we are all of us, men and women alike, always capable of being both the best and worst of lovers—unpredictably, circumstantially, regardless of technical finesse, and, finally and sadly, without regard to common sense. How many women I've wished the sex could be better with (because I've known that in other ways they were not only good people, but good for me)? How many times have I actually wished the sex were bad with someone (because I've known she was, in other respects, bad for me)? Which is another motto to pin up on your wall: "Good Sex Is Not Necessarily an Omen of a Good Life."

Something Zipless
This Way Comes

You will find no word spoken here against what Dudley Moore, that fine, funny actor, recently called "the meaningful one-night stand." I think you will find no word spoken against that great institution anywhere these days by anyone not identified elsewhere in the copy as a "religious leader" or "church spokesman." Which is not to say that all of us, men and women alike, are not hopeful, ever hopeful, that something a little more lasting will evolve from that first sexual encounter. Women, indeed, may still be—liberated or no—a tiny tad more hopeful in this regard than we are. But, after all, we owe to a woman—Erica Jong—the most colorful phrase describing this briefest of brief encounters: the zipless fuck.

The implication of Ms. Jong's—pardon me—seminal work, the whole drift of sexual life these days, is toward a recognition of the fact that at a certain basic level man and woman are quite alike in their needs. We are all, at various times, lonely in ways that cannot be assuaged by a night at the ball game with the guys from the office, an evening at the movies with the girls from the same place. There is also a recognition that in certain circumstances a woman can be just as curious as we are to discover what a particular member of the opposite sex might be like in bed. And everyone is discovering that, despite Ms. Jong's failure to go very deeply into this aspect of ziplessness, despite the one-night stand's bad reputation in certain circles (and despite what all of us feel bound to declare about this matter on public occasions), a single night of love can be a tender and even, in memory, a rather poignant experience. Some relationships, in fact, have a natural life that is—or should be—of just this brief duration. And they come to grief only because one or more of the parties to them insist on trying to extend them beyond their proper, perhaps preordained, span.

Mind, I'm not saying that life should be a succession of one-nighters. Quite the opposite; if you find yourself falling into that pattern, particularly after you've been separated for a while, you probably ought to give some serious thought to the situation. Maybe even consider seeking out some professional guidance, hmm?

But every once in a while you will run into one of those times in which one night of love is, when clearly viewed in the next morning's light, sufficient unto everyone's curiosity, randiness, or travel schedule, and a polite and pleasant disengagement—no hurt feelings, but no false promises, either—is in order. It is the distinguishing characteristic, or one of them, anyway, of the sensitive and experienced lover (of either sex) that he or she can recognize this small, not entirely sad fact of life and act discreetly upon it.

If that seems painfully obvious to you, well and good. But I must confess that it was not all that clear to me in the early days of my singleness, for, child of the fifties that I was, I continued to harbor the notion that if I took a woman to bed, something of great and terrible consequence had occurred. Of course, it had—I continue to cling to that belief. But that does not necessarily imply that everyone has to spend the next six months dealing with it. Sometimes a bunch of flowers and a nice note will do. And bring a great sigh of relief to the recipient as a fringe benefit. Don't worry; you'll catch on. I think.

Lies, Lies, Lies

The zipless spirit can become chronic. It can extend for weeks, months, years, even in some advanced cases for a lifetime. And it is easy enough to rationalize. Did not Chairman Mao himself advise us to let a hundred flowers bloom? And is it not right to be good little gardeners, gathering rosebuds while we may? Especially now—when we are so newly escaped from the briar patch, which any declining marriage is bound to resemble toward the end?

Besides, it's such fun. One fellow I know still likes to talk about the time he had seven different women in eight days on two coasts—one of whom inveigled him into an experimental visit to Plato's Retreat, that romper room for adults, where they discovered—big deal—that they actually could get it on in public, and from which they emerged with many amusing social notes. (Did you know, for example, that the management orders out for pizza promptly at midnight?) Another chap I know likes to muse about the time he went to bed with one lady in the afternoon, played three sets of tennis with her afterward, and then took her best friend out for dinner that evening, with delightful postprandial results. In later life these are the sort of exploits aging roués like to cackle over in their chimney corners while they watch the young people having fun. And probably they are, for some among the congregation, a necessity. We'd feel sort of left out of things—out of step with the spirit of the age, don't you know?—if we didn't acquire a few good, basic tales of sexual athleticism to relate when the port's going around and the conversation dips down into the libidinal.

But there is, obviously, an absurd side to an action-packed life. I will pass quickly over the health problems it presents. Crabs, for example, are funny enough when they happen to somebody else, but the joke tends to wear a little thin when you're the guy with all your bed linen in the laundry and most of your nice clothes in for a dry cleaning. ("Ah, er, do you think I can have twenty-four-hour service on those?") And that, of course, is only the mildest method nature has of warning us to slow down.

About the social and psychological costs of the life of a sexual Scarlet Pimpernel, I'd like to go into a little more cautionary detail. To begin with—for that matter, to begin *and* end with—there's the lying. We all know that an element of mystery is essential to the conduct of human affairs, especially human love affairs. But you're going to find that there's entirely too much of this good thing if you're bouncing from bed to bed to bed.

Take, for example, the simplest imaginable case. You've been sleeping happily with someone for a few weeks, and then, one night, you go to party and, sure enough, over there in the corner, talking to that short little round-faced guy, is this willowy creature with long blonde hair and the nicest smile—something about it is both shy and knowing all at once—and what can you do? You sort of slide over there when the Lou Costello lookalike goes off in search of a drink, and you ascertain, besides her name, rank, and serial number, the fact that old Lou is just somebody she used to know when she roomed with his cousin Anne. More delicate exploration ensues, and it becomes clear that she is not inseparably attached to anyone, and that you have two or three friends in common (which guarantees to you both that class, education, or what-have-you differences are not going to arise immediately and make trouble). It is, of course, vulgar to whip out your notepad and pen at this point and start taking down her name and phone number. That is why society invented the institution of calling your hostess the next morning to thank her for a lovely evening. In the course of exercising this bit of *politesse,* you casually get the pretty lady's phone number.

Whereupon you fall into a guilty funk. Because there is really nothing wrong with your present arrangement, no reason at all to start stepping out on it. Except—natch—you're curious and maybe a little restless, with all those prehistoric hunter-gatherer instincts buzzing away inside you. Besides, all the promises you've made to your present companion were, well, unspoken. So you call your new friend. And you make a date. And things go well. And now you're in the soup. Because, really, you like both of these ladies and don't see why you can't enjoy them both equally.

Well, you can't—not for any length of time, anyway. I don't care how nice and casual you keep it with both of them, after a time each is going to think—and quite rightly, too—that she has some modest claim on you, which includes a perfect right to inquire where you were when one of them decided to call you last night around 11:30. (And don't try telling anyone you were so tired you just decided to turn off the phone or, even more lamely, that you've been having some trouble with it and were just about to call your service representative.) We live in an age when no one, absolutely no one, was born yesterday.

Based on such goodwill as you've accumulated, you'll probably get through that first little white lie. People—you among them, when the situation is reversed—would generally prefer not to have their worst fears confirmed. But there'll come a time ... I mean, how can you *know* ten days in advance that you are required to work late at the office—on a Saturday?—when she calls to invite you to a party? What do you *mean,* the entire weekend is shot? And so forth. Of course, if you add still more affairs to your busy social calendar, your problems are going to double, treble ... and start heading for calculus.

Sigh. I don't know why I bothered to write all that down. You're not going to listen. You're not going to listen because a man's gotta do what a man's gotta do, and all that stuff. I suppose there's something in that. Just once in this life I imagine all of us have got to indulge our Don Juan fantasies, see what it's like, for once, to have golden problems. So go ahead. But remember, once is enough. And if you keep getting into these messes, don't come running to me.

Seems to Me I've Heard That Song Before

Let us assume that, for once, you've learned your lesson, that having discovered the Don's downside, you have become a more conservative trustee of your own romantic fortunes, that you are, in fact, that most charming of antique legal fictions, "the prudent man." You therefore conduct your affairs not as some manic conglomerateur, but as a sensible enterpriser of the classic stripe, closing the books on your previous venture before investigating new investment opportunities. Serial profligacy, you naturally—and somewhat smugly—assume is less taxing than the simultaneous variety.

But do not settle back too quickly on your cushion of moral superiority, for it will come upon the prudent man, even as it does the imprudent one, that most dismal of reckonings, that terrible moment of truth that causes more philanderers to opt for early retirement than any other: that heart-stopping, mouth-shutting instant when, leaning close to light her cigarette, fully appreciative of the perfume of her hair, the glow of the candles reflected in her eyes, a voice intrudes. At first you try to shut it out of consciousness, but there is something naggingly familiar about it, some intonation or rhythm that puts you vaguely, annoyingly in mind of something that is tiresomely familiar. You pause, you tuck your brandy snifter between middle and index fingers, gently rolling the liquid inside, as Charles Boyer so entrancingly did in the movies of yesteryear. You stare thoughtfully into it, trying to hide your panic. For the voice that has just come through, loud and clear, is your own, and the awful realization that has struck you is that you've heard this line of yours before, *and that you are sick to death of it.*

Let us recall Willy Loman to the stand. Remember how he feared the moment when a spot on his suit, a lack of shine on his shoes, would betray his pretensions to confidence, that air of well-being so essential to his successful canvassing of New England? Well, Ace, once again you have reason to know how Willy felt. Those wryly deprecatory little anecdotes, in which you emerge as such a civilized and humorous fellow—now they sound idiotic. Those Wildean epigrams, so neatly summarizing the current state of the sexual battleground—what nonsense. Those attentive little queries, so sweetly solicitous of her views and her general well-being—surely she sees through them. The trouble is, you've been here before—too many times, with too many ladies. You know all the moves, and the end game, too. And now, as you contemplate them you can't help be struck by this thought: Falsity, falsity, all is falsity.

Maybe yes, maybe no—realistically speaking. But as Old Willy would also have been glad to tell you, you can't sell anyone anything if you cannot first sell yourself on it, and once your critical faculties start homing in on your line, once you begin boring yourself with it, there is but a hop, skip, and jump before you start boring other people with it.

And, I might add, even if you're entirely immune to self-awareness of that sort, you can't help but grow weary of the whole dating process: picking just the shirt and tie combination—not too raffish, not too stiffish—that will strike exactly the right note with this latest stranger; selecting the restaurant that will neither overwhelm nor underwhelm her; making sure it takes American Express; standing on the street corner afterward, dancing a gavotte around the her-place/your-place question (and then wondering, should your place win out, if the breakfast dishes are still in the sink). *Quel* drag.

Now, you're going to recover from the first few attacks of this sort; but sooner or later you're going have to face facts— as a roué, you are now approaching terminal status. After all, you're not really that kind of a man, are you? A guy putting notches in his holster or his belt or wherever? Most of us aren't—it's just too damned exhausting. And, in the end, unsatisfying.

The Legend of the Beth-El Home

Before considering the alternatives to your present randomly randy life-style—let us pause for a moment to consider the one reason not to make a change. That is, pure panic. Three or four years ago I was sitting around with one of my best friends, chap I'll call Bernie. We had both, so we thought, passed through the stage of trying to make out with anything that moved and were attempting to turn our minds toward higher things, an effort initially not crowned with enormous success.

"Ah, the hell with it, Bernie," I said. "There are some people who just shouldn't settle down."

"????"

"I mean, probably we're just not the types."

"We've gotta," said Bernie. He spoke with considerable intensity.

Now it was my turn. "????"

"I don't want to end up in the Beth-El Home."

He was referring to a nursing home he passed every day on the way to work. Outside, when the weather was good, its inmates could be seen, their awful lightweight metal and plastic chairs lined up on the sidewalk, backs literally to the wall, so their occupants could warm their lonely old bones in the sun.

According to Bernie, they never seemed to be talking to one another, or even to themselves. They just turned vacantly toward the heat. No one, it seemed, was organizing cribbage games for them. Or even laying on some milk and cookies.

It is, I admit, a terrible vision. And something to which we all ought to pay some sympathetic heed. But not for selfish reasons. First of all, whatever we do with our sunset years, the chances are very good that our last bed will be a single bed and we might as well prepare for that gloomy eventuality—at least in some corner of our mind. But more to the immediate point, it is foolish to force yourself—and someone else, naturally—into a settled, perhaps final, relationship merely to avoid the oncoming express train of loneliness. Or worse, because you require a little home nursing. God knows, a little home nursing would be nice after you've lived alone for a while—breakfast on the table, dirty shirts in the machine, a supply of Stresstabs constantly replenished by other hands. But to be the prisoner of that need, to think that you can't forever live alone and like it—that's selling yourself short. And worse, it leads to a kind of selfish imposition on someone else, someone you're actually only pretending to love in return for services rendered. That seems to me nothing less than immoral.

And, besides, where is it written that every relationship must follow the same pattern—you meet, you get intimate, you move in together, you live that way the rest of your lives? Your friends, of course, are going to expect you to follow that pattern. *They* did, after all, and are anxious to see others sharing their pleasure, or their pain—however it worked out for them. But you don't have to. After all, Jean-Paul Sartre and Simone de Beauvoir were together for several decades and neither gave up his or her apartment. I know another couple who were faithfully involved with one another—as close in their profound and enviable intimacy as anyone I've heard about—despite the fact that they lived on separate continents. The only problem was paying for all the airplane tickets required to effect their apparently delicious meetings. We hear all the time, these days, of couples who have jobs in widely separated cities and meet only on weekends—but contentedly so. All I'm saying is that endless proximity is no longer a requisite for a good relationship. Just because that's what most people have, it doesn't mean you have to have it— or even that it will turn out to be right for you. So don't let custom dictate to you if you don't feel like it.

None of the foregoing is to be taken as a prescription. All I'm saying is that there *are* options. As for my pal Bernie, little old traditionalist that he is, he lucked out. He met a terrific lady, and, not long after our little exchange, they happily settled down together in what appears to all their friends to be a state of permanent, and exemplary, bliss. Gives hope to us all.

Picky, Picky, Picky

I don't mean to imply that the minute you sense your roguish days are drawing to an end, you must rush into the first promise of permanence that presents itself. Indeed, it may be that when you feel the legs going—when they just don't have their old spring as they make their weekly or monthly hop into a new sack—you may wish to indulge yourself in a cooling-off period, take stock, and otherwise enjoy that trendy phenomenon known as "the new celibacy." I'm going to save lengthy discussion of its pleasures and perils for later, because there is a time, a bit further along in your story, when it is going to be even more useful (not to say essential) for you. For the moment let it merely be noted that it need not necessarily be regarded as a pastime akin to hitting yourself over the head with a hammer. It *does* feel good when it stops, but it also has its psychic uses. It is a time when you can measure not only how far you've come, but how far you want to go, or think you dare aspire to go in the course of your changing and, yes, developing life. Besides which, all of us need a break from our routines, especially the sexual ones.

If, now, you are sensible enough (A) to have ceased to regard sex as the most exhilarating form of contact sport and (B) to have learned to avoid entangling alliances motivated solely by your own whimpering need for a Nanny, then it stands to reason that the only thing you have left to worry about is (C).

(C) is—what else?—the fear of commitment. Now, as somebody or other used to say, I want to make one thing perfectly clear, and that is that I'm not talking marriage here. I'm *never* talking marriage. Don't see any point to it, since I've already done my bit to propagate the race. If you're in that position why would you want to do something that just makes a lot of paperwork for the lawyers and accountants to fool around with expensively? But, all right, *de gustibus*—a lot of people aren't happy until they've formalized their arrangements in some way. If you're one of those, go ahead. I'm not stopping you.

But if deep in my essentially anarchical heart I believe legalisms are a waste of time when life is just one damned unpredictable contingency after another, that doesn't mean I'm opposed to a man and a woman making a commitment, an endlessly renewable (like every day) commitment to one another. As a matter of fact, I think it is, finally, the only way to live.

So, to put the matter simply, after you've had your fun and games, and after you've digested the experience, go for it. Now, the first funny thing you're going to realize is is that the lady you choose to make this scary experiment with probably won't look so very different from the others, probably won't be doing anything all that much more amusing with her life, probably will not be all *that* remarkable or distinctive. If you're honest about it you'll realize, as you start to settle down, that you might just as well have done so with about a half-dozen other ladies you previously bailed out on for some not very good reason or another. This is known as one of life's little ironies. Nothing to do but shake your head over it. Timing, in these matters, is everything—as I can't repeat often enough. And timing—the coincidence of her mood and your mood—is something none of us has any control over.

Be that as it may, simple common sense, in matters of the heart, does not come easily to most of us, and some among the congregation are going to go right on rejecting, however sweetly and pleasantly, all kinds of people they should not treat in so cavalier a fashion, leaving behind them a trail of hearts not so much broken as puzzled. I'm certain I have been such a one myself, and I think it is a disagreeable way to be, an abuse of your new-found privileges.

I'm really not contradicting myself; I still think its right and natural to embrace as much experience as you can when first the marital bonds are broken. I'm well aware of the basic rationalization for extending that period: you're exercising suitable caution, you're taking your time, looking carefully around until you find a woman about whom you don't have even a single, minor, unformed, unspoken reservation.

And you know what I say to that? I say you're bananas. For what you are expressing is a kind of idealism that can only be termed feckless. Nobody, as you may have heard, is perfect—least of all you, fella—and it would be a good idea if you admitted that there's something absurd about your sitting around behind your pot belly complaining that Judy's ankles are just a smidgen too thick for you to accept her as your life's partner. Or that Jenny's chest is just a wee mite flat to please you in your impeccability. Or that Jackie looks as if she's going to have a cellulite problem when she hits 40.

I won't even mention—not in a work that could fall into the hands of the innocent and impressionable—some of the more intimate imperfections that acquaintances of mine have alluded to as excuses for bailing out of relationships just when they got going kinda nice and promising, but I've heard some dillies. And they have led me to the conclusion that at least on this one point the hard-shelled feminists are right: on the whole men far too readily objectify and fetishize women. You can blame the movies, advertising, gatefold magazines, the whole damn-fool culture if you want to, but in the end you have to blame yourself for going along with the prevailing nonsense. "Beauty," said Stendhal, "is only the promise of happiness." It is not to be mistaken for the genuine article.

And this physiological nit-picking is merely symbolic of all the other little difficulties we direct our attention to when we're looking for a way out. So she snores. Or her underwear runs toward the boringly sensible when you have something a little more Frenchified in mind. Or she has this budgie bird to which she is unreasonably devoted. Or she likes to go to revivals of Jeanette MacDonald–Nelson Eddy movies. Whatever.

Yeah, these little eccentricities could symbolize deeper incompatibilities. But maybe—probably—they don't symbolize much of anything. They are just ... well ... eccentricities, like your having to close all the closet doors before you go to sleep. Or lining up all the stuff on your desk geometrically. Or collecting first editions of the works of Erle Stanley Gardner, all of which you doubtless regard—correctly—as part of your singularity, parts of the adorable whole that makes you you. Certainly you can see that her little quirks and oddities are the same. If you can't, you'd better go somewhere and take tolerance lessons.

Because, sport, this is only the beginning. For no matter how hard you try to avoid it, eventually you're going to find yourself drawn into the realm of more serious relationships, the kind that begin ordinarily enough but then develop lengthy middle passages and, of course, endings of various kinds. Once you're embarked on one of those relationships you're going to have so many real problems to contend with that these little defensive ploys we've been talking about are going to be seen for exactly what they are: child's play. As a matter of fact, there will come a time—and very shortly, at that—when you're going to look back on them with a certain amount of nostalgia.

Symbolic Acts, Real Feelings

Some years ago, Mary McCarthy wrote a short story—it reappeared later in *The Group*—about the symbolic meaning and practical consequences of a woman's leaving her diaphragm at her lover's apartment. It was a witty story, and rather scandalous when it showed up in *Partisan Review* in the 1950s, since in those years ladies were not supposed to discuss such matters in public. The act of committing that pessary to the man's medicine cabinet was, McCarthy implied, roughly the equivalent of accepting an engagement ring—or, anyway, a fraternity pin—in gentler times.

Still is, of course. But the world moves on, and there are other gestures, proposals, questions that are not to be taken lightly either, and you should be aware of them, especially as you move on—on to less transient affairs, affairs that seriously test your feelings and those of the women who bring to mind for you those stray fantasies of permanence we are all always prey to. What follows is not to be construed as a warning. Almost everybody, I guess, must eventually settle down, or so we have been conditioned to believe. But you must understand the implications of certain seemingly inconsequential acts, which actually carry a fairly heavy symbolic weight, and which you should not propose unless you are really serious about the lady. And should not accept lightly if they are proposed to you.

Let's begin at the beginning. Let's imagine that things have gone absolutely swimmingly on the first date—all sorts of delicious electricity in the air. (Is there any more delicious ambiance in this world than that of a dinner table at which a man and a woman simultaneously become aware that in a matter of half-hours they will be happily, excitedly in bed together?) Let's imagine, too, no foolish delays having been brooked, that sex has turned out to be every bit as pleasant as you both imagined it would be. The question now arises (depending on the venue, naturally): do you spend the night? Does she? Most of the time, the answer is self-evident. For example, she has children and you don't want to confront a sea of questioning little faces over your morning cornflakes. Or, conversely, if you are at your place, she really has to get home to relieve the baby sitter. But if there are no obvious impediments to all-night cosiness, this is the first of several gray areas through which you will have to grope your way.

Now, traditionally it has been women, believing more firmly than men in the consequentiality of the sexual act, who have opposed hit-and-run tactics, who tend to want to snuggle down for the night. But that is no longer one of life's universals. Nowadays the woman, quite as often as the man, finds that she does not wish to confront him—and herself—by dawn's early light.

Here once again, discretion seems to me the better part of valor. People digest experience at different rates, and at different levels of pleasure and regret. If she starts talking about the breakfast meeting with an important client that she's forgotten until this very moment, then there may be some wisdom in pretending that she's just reminded you that, by golly, you have a nine o'clock staff meeting yourself.

(It may also be that, even as you discuss such quotidian

matters, a mood of *tristesse* will overcome you, and that the thought of making a graceful exit—even if the weather outside *is* frightful—has a certain appeal. If so, you should act on that impulse—especially if her protestations ring purely *pro forma* in your ears. Again, these are courtesies that adults should be able to extend to one another without hard feelings.)

I need hardly add—at least I *hope* I need hardly add—that if you really do have a staff meeting at some ungodly hour and she makes it clear that she is going to feel ill-used if you leave, then, as a gentleman, you are honor-bound to stay. It's all right—only a handful of the staff will actually notice that you're wearing yesterday's coat and tie, and their curiosity about this sartorial lapse will doubtless be tinctured by a certain envy.

By this time, being the experienced chap you are, you will understand that, on the whole, first nights tend to come off rather well. The sense of risk mutually taken and mutually rewarded; the first shared fantasies of good times yet to come; the pillow talk that flows so much more easily now that the sexual hurdle has been safely negotiated, revealing new mutualities of likes and dislikes—all of these generally lead to a desire to snuggle down comfortably and relax. Or maybe to murmur away a happily sleepless night. But it may be up to you, if you have some honest doubts about just where all this is going to lead, to suggest a momentary disengagement. That, too, is part of being a gentleman—not allowing false hopes, or premature hopes, to build up.

Making judgments of this kind—is it the real turtle soup, or only the mock?—requires, as you can see, tact, delicacy, finesse. And experience. For remember, you will be making them at a moment when your defenses are down and your hopes are up. These days, thank God, you will get more assistance from women in making them than was formerly the case. But you've both got to keep your wits about you. Because, for a while, things aren't going to get any easier.

For what inescapably follows upon the successful negotiation of the overnight question is the matter of the weekend. Sometimes it follows with shocking suddenness, as in Saturday morning following Friday night. It may be that you had some secret hopes in that direction. In which case, all well and good. But it may also be that you had other plans, which you'd just as soon not discuss over bagels and the *Times*. This, of course, is where your children come in handy. You can always invoke their scheduled noontime visit as an excuse for shooting out someone you really don't fancy a gallery trot in SoHo with just yet. Even if they have gone off to the lake with Mom. But that sort of thing is small potatoes. What I'm talking about is The Weekend—that planned, hoped for, dreaded first test of the higher compatibility.

It usually begins with an innocent question: "God, wouldn't you love to just get out of the city for a little while?" To which the natural response is, "Sure." I mean, we'd all like to get out of the city for a little while, wouldn't we? But, be careful. Be careful in asking the question, and be careful in answering it. For you're not talking about weekends like you and your late spouse used to take, where you gratefully dumped the kids on Grandma's doorstep and indulged yourself in the erotic refreshment that a strange hotel or motel room can provide the chronically married couple.

No, what you're talking about is one of the major testing grounds of a modern relationship. For what you're immediately going to get into is some very heavy stuff: seashore vs. the mountains, active (i.e., skiing) vs. passive (i.e., curling up with a couple of good books in a picturesque inn). Not to mention actually sharing a bathroom—and you know how thin walls and doors are lately—for a couple of days. And maybe even a really shocking proposal or two. To wit:

WEST COAST LOVELY: The desert is so lovely this time of year.
ME: Never been.
WCL: I know this great little ranch. Individual cottages. Terrific dining room ...
ME: Sounds nice.
WCL: We could drop some acid.
ME: Huh??
WCL: I've always wanted to turn you on.
ME: Gosh, maybe as soon as I deliver those revisions ...
WCL: I'll bet you've never even done acid.

That's right, I haven't. And dope makes me sleepy. And coke keeps me awake. And, above all, I wasn't about to share a mystical experience—or worse, a bad trip—with a virtual stranger.

You take my point, I hope. Maybe if our relationship had been allowed to prosper for a while longer, and if, at something like the same moment, a desire to share those deeper intimacies that go well beyond the sexual, had come upon us, I might have taken her up on the offer. But it was too much too soon. I mean, I hadn't even introduced her to my tennis partners yet.

Or, to put the matter a little more seriously, and a little more generally, each affair has a rhythm of its own, and a very good way to test its viability is to see if the idea of certain pleasantries and conveniences occur at more or less the same time to both of you. Do not back off a proposal for a weekend—or even for allowing her to leave a change of clothes in your closet—if that seems natural and right to you. But if the timing seems wrong, then the correct thing to say—nicely—is: "The timing seems wrong."

Naturally, the converse applies. There is going to come a moment when it will seem very pleasant and civilized if you could just buy a dressing gown and hang it in her closet so you don't have to get all dressed just to enjoy your morning cup of coffee in leisure and decency. If she changes the subject when you make that suggestion, then back off, for God's sake. There'll come a time when she buys one for you and presents it ceremoniously. Or she never will. Either way, you'll know where you stand. And that's what this section has been all about—making sure you're both standing in more or less the same place at the same time.

We all have movies running in our heads in which we have the star part. You shouldn't run around casting people in the lead opposite you without making sure they're up to the role. By the same token you don't want to get into someone else's picture without being certain that the part is right for you.

Remember the Bower Bird

But all right — you've made your decision. What you want is a co-starring role, billing above the title, the whole shot, in her movie. Trouble is, she isn't at all sure about that casting. Yes, she's moved you up from the bit she originally had you in. You've very definitely got a featured part. But the lead ... ?

If you find yourself in that circumstance, it might be a good idea to try a new metaphor. For example, we are told—especially if we happen to be living with lovely, romantic ladies of cosmopolitan interests while we are preparing manuscripts of this character—about the peculiarly winning ways of the male of the Australian species mentioned above. It is his habit, when he goes courting, to wing about collecting bits of bone, shell, and flora, which he then arranges in a neat semicircle on the ground. He is said to afford a rather comic and touching sight as he steps back from this collection, eyeing it carefully to see if it pleases his esthetic sense, then fussily rearranging the display until it seems exactly right to him. But only when it is perfectly in order does he conduct his intended to this little exhibition, which the *Oxford Dictionary* quaintly refers to as, a "place of resort." Within it, he does a little mating dance, intended to wow the female, and only after he has performed to her satisfaction does she consent to whatever unmentionable behavior comes next in Bower Bird's mating ritual.

Now, if some starling hanging around in the Australian outback doesn't find it inconvenient to go to all this trouble to prove his interest in a member of the opposite sex, neither should you. And, I'm not talking flowers and candy and little impulsive surprises that catch your fancy on the way home from the office. Those should go without saying, it should go without saying. I'm talking about romantic gestures on a grand scale.

For example, I recently heard of a man who lived in France, had some business in New York, and had a lady he was terribly smitten with in Los Angeles. It was unbearable to him that he should be on the same continent with her and not see her. But, alas, his schedule was tight and hers was impossible. What he did, however, was call her, tell her to meet him at the Los Angeles airport and then hop on a plane. He was able to spend just 45 minutes with her, billing and cooing under the glare of the waiting-room fluorescents, then catch the next plane back. It was, the recipient of this splendid gesture has since told me, the single most romantic thing that has ever happened to her.

Another friend of mine, some years ago, was courting an extraordinarily beautiful ballerina when he was suddenly called out of town on business of indeterminate duration. He told his beloved that he would not inform her precisely of his return, but that she would not be in any doubt about his arrival; there would be a signal she couldn't miss. And so there was. For he went straight from his train to a flower shop, where he purchased not just a bouquet or two, but every damned posy in the place. That night, when she was taking her curtain calls, a bunch of messengers trouped down the aisles and simply carpeted the stage with his offering.

Another guy I knew had a lady in London and a job to do

on the Great Barrier Reef in Australia. When the job was done, it would have been possible for him to fly back to the States the way he had gone, that is, back across the Pacific. But he discovered that it was equally possible to continue on around the world, via Perth and Bombay, and stop off in London. He, too, was on a tight schedule, but by sitting upright on the plane for 28 consecutive hours, he was able to gain 24 hours and spend them with his dear heart in London. That he spent most of them falling asleep in theaters and restaurants and even in the very place he most wanted to be awake—namely, her bed—was of less consequence to her than the fact that he had made this supreme effort.

Now my point is not that great swooping gestures of this kind can make overpowering first impressions on women. As a matter of fact, that's not my point at all. I mean, were you to attempt one of them too soon in a relationship, you would run the risk of making a damn fool of yourself. No, the time for such goings-on is a bit later, when you've gotten through the preliminaries and both parties are taking stock, wondering if this thing is for real or not. It's at that moment, if you judge this to be nothing less than an affair to remember and, just maybe, a once-in-a-lifetime probability, that you must take fate by the hand and attempt to seal the bargain by flying expensively and surprisingly to her side. Or something.

But there's another reason to go to all that trouble, and it has nothing to do with overwhelming your lady love. It has to do with the way you look at yourself. By which I mean that if, like most of us, you've spent most of your life routinely getting and spending, paying the school bills and keeping the orthodontist at bay, and generally being a sober and reliable citizen, you probably have a fairly dull image of yourself. A plodder. A guy who's brought too many of his clothes at the semiannual sales and ordered out to the deli for too many lunches at his desk. Secretly, in your heart of hearts, you've always known that you were capable of acting like the hero of an old-fashioned romantic movie. It's just that what with one thing and another, you've never got around to it.

Well here's your big chance. And even if you have to ask American Express to spread the payments over the next twelve months, go for it. And once having risked it, you'll find this new capacity for demonstrating feelings on an international scale will change your image of yourself, and your feelings about yourself. That corned-beef-on-rye-hold-the-mustard will never again taste quite so cardboardy.

Finally, and this is really the heart of the matter, when you emulate the Bower Bird, you will find the flip side of the caution I counseled earlier—all that stuff about being careful when it comes to weekending prematurely and so on. If caution is part of your repertoire, then incaution must be, too. Because it will give your relationship a grounding in a moment of historical wonder, the reverberations of which will help you both through whatever bad patches that lie ahead, a dimly whispered melody over there in memory's oboe section that every couple needs to be able to hear amid the brass and percussion of life in our times. Even if, finally, the relationship fails, even if the parting is ugly and stupid, neither of you will ever totally erase a memory of the quality we've been talking about. When she reads about your promotion in the paper, she may at least sigh wistfully over what might have been. When you read about her wedding in the same journal, you may at least wish her well. All in all, I'd say you can't lose when by creating a good impression you also create a good memory.

What About the Children?

There are two kinds of children in this world—hers and yours—and just when you think you've built your bower, just when you're ready to settle down to a little happiness of your own—and you've both earned it by this time, no kidding—you're going to have to spare a thought for the bairns. And it's going to have to be a careful one, too, by God. For the statistics tell us that if a third of the kids sail through the breakup of a marriage unscathed, another third of them are quite seriously disturbed for a time, while the last third are more or less permanently scarred by the experience. And, kids being kids, it is not always easy to tell which group the ones you are dealing with belong to.

Which doesn't mean that you are not going to be confronted by some rather comic spectacles as you enter this phase of a relationship. I once had an extremely nice affair with an extremely nice woman who happened to have an extremely nice 8-year-old son. I was properly introduced to him, I spent a good deal of time chatting him up while she made the last fixes on her hair before going out on a date, we even took him along occasionally to dinner or on outings, getting him used to my presence.

Finally, there came a night when we decided it would be

okay if I slept over, that my presence at the breakfast table next morning would not unduly shock the youngster. But my friend arose earlier than I did, and the first thing I was conscious of by dawn's early light, was a cold, wet nose sniffing around my exposed toes. "Go away, doggie," I muttered, not yet fully awake to the fact that where doggie went his owner was sure to follow. Adrenaline zinged through my nervous system, for it is one thing to find a fully dressed man in the breakfast nook, quite another to find him naked in Mommy's bed. Clutching the sheet around me, I bolted upright and, sure enough, there was the household's last remaining resident male, regarding me soberly. He spoke before I could, and this is what he said: "Dick, do you always wear your watch to bed?"

There ensued an informative chat about people's funny sleeping habits. Clearly, what we were dealing with here was one of the happy one-third, and a couple of days later I bought him the catcher's mitt he had had his eye on in the local sporting goods store.

All well and good, and you can count yourself a lucky fellow if the strange kids who turn up in your new life are all in latency. You can also count yourself lucky if your new friend is the mother of girls, who seem mainly to want to live vicariously through Mom's new romance. If what you encounter are adolescent boys, then, alas, you are going to have an awful lot of sullen conversations in the months ahead. Because they take a highly protective, not to say insanely jealous, view of Mom. Here, for instance, is a typical telephone conversation:

> KID: Hello.
> YOU: Oh, hi, Calvin. Your mother home?
> KID: Nah.
> YOU: When do you expect her?
> KID: Don't know.

YOU: Well, tell her I called. I'm at . . .
TELEPHONE: Click.

Your face-to-face confrontations are likely to be equally brief. Indeed, for many months an adolescent boy is likely to appear more or less as a blur passing through the living room when you come to call. Or, if it is later in the evening, he is probably going to do his poltergeist imitation. Even though The Young Master has retired, you are likely to discover that every time you start to slip your arm around Mom there will arise a great thumping and crashing from some other part of the house. To be followed by the heavy tread of footsteps heading for the kitchen and a midnight snack. Or there will be alarming coughings and snortlings as his asthma picks this particular moment to act up.

There is nothing to be done about this. It may be that, for reasons having nothing to do with him, Calvin will simply disappear from your life. If not, you must simply be patient. Do not offer to take him to the ball game or give him tickets to a rock concert prematurely. Do not attempt to ingratiate yourself with conversations about sports or schoolwork or girls until his mother indicates he's ready for something more than a cross and preoccupied hello. Above all, don't get into guilt trips. All you can do is wait the little bastard out. Ultimately, he will accept you because he has to accept you; children tend to be highly realistic about these things. And assuming you are, by nature, agreeable, tolerant and not particularly uptight, you ought to be able to establish a pleasant enough relationship with the new kids in your life. On this point it is probably well to bear in mind the words of a wise old shrink who once told me, "Step-parents don't count." By which he meant that you are automatically excused from participation in the Freudian dramas of other people's children, even if you are seeing them every day. Which is nice, because you cannot obtain an honorable discharge from that participation in your own kids' lives, and enough is enough.

About your own little Oedipuses and Electras, you will have to exercise a certain care and discretion. The chances are that, at least at first, your kids will live with their mother and that they will be frightfully curious about how you are doing, and what you are doing, in your new single life. It is so painfully obvious that you are divorced from their mother, not them, that it seems superfluous to remind you of that fact. But I run into so many men who seem to have abandoned their children along with their ex-wives—they seem to remind these guys of past unpleasantnesses and inadequacies—that I feel I must tell you, as firmly as I can: *don't do that.*

Kids can be a drag every once in a while when you're leading a happy new life as a single male—reminding you at awkward moments that you're not quite as carefree as you like to think you are. But they are also a living link with your past, and the need for continuity is among the most powerful of your needs at this juncture, whether you admit it or not. Also, remember this: theirs is the love that endures forever, if you give it half a chance. You can count on it as you can count on little else in this life.

Beyond that, you have just been given a terrific opportunity, which you would be an idiot to pass up. That, of course, is the chance to reconstitute your relationship with your children, to give them time that is uncluttered by the complications that surely attended the last unhappy years of your marriage. It is really the best of the new starts you can now make, and I feel—despite various ups and downs, various awkwardnesses and insensitivities on my part—that I'm a better parent to my kids now than I was when we all lived distractedly under the same roof. Absence should make a father's heart grow fonder. If it doesn't then you are some kind of moral monster.

Which is not to say that I didn't make mistakes. I think I let too much of my pain and anger show in the first months of separation. I'm sure I was far too volubly critical of their mother in those days than I should have been in their presence. Try to skip all that if you can. It's confusing and it doesn't do anybody any good. You're just going to feel stupid and indiscreet in the aftermath of one of these outbursts.

I'm also convinced that you must not too quickly start bringing your kids into contact with the new woman in your life. About that, at least, I was terribly discreet, and glad of it, now that I look back. Obviously, one of the advantages that a male generally has over a female in this situation is precisely that—for the most part—his kids do not live with him; thus he does not have to introduce them to every idiot who comes calling, which, obviously, a woman who has custody of the kids must do. So it was not until my youngest child expressed, through her mother, a certain concern about me—"What would happen if Daddy got sick? Who'd take care of him?"—that I presented the children with the lady I was then involved with. By lucky coincidence, that happened to be a serious and long-lasting relationship, she was an extremely sensitive and decent woman, and, as a matter of fact, she and the children are still friends (as, indeed, she and I still are).

Not every single and childless woman is as wise as she was. Some try to measure your intentions toward them by your willingness to introduce them to your children. If you delay it, they begin to entertain dark imaginings that you find them unworthy of this presentation, that you have somehow judged them lacking in motherly—actually, step-motherly—qualities. I read recently in a newspaper column that some women of this type take to leaving little objects around the man's apartment—a scarf or a bit of jewelry—as if to stake out a territorial claim on it, hoping that the kids will get the message. That is, I think, reprehensible. Patience is everything in matters of these kind, and if you cannot quell her impatience, you may perhaps want to rethink the whole thing. I mean, what's her hurry?

The same thing applies to her relationship with the kids after she has met them. She should not press too quickly for big-sisterly intimacy. She should not shower them with gifts and favors. And certainly she should not enlist their aid—"Wouldn't it be wonderful if your father settled down again?"—in cementing her relationship with you. In short, the standards you would apply to yourself in dealing with the children of someone you've come to care about apply equally to someone who professes to care about you and yours. Gentleness, humor, a capacity to recall what it was like to be a kid yourself, an awareness that these are tricky times for anyone's kids, even if their home is not a "broken" one, and above all, simple human understanding—these are the watchwords. But I don't mean to frighten you. All the women I've come far enough with to introduce to my kids have turned out to be terrific with them. For the rest—well, our lack of mutual terrificness obviated the problem.

Jaws, or, "My God, It Just Came Out of Nowhere"

Okay. That's it. Everyone's all settled down. No more problems. Guess this book must be almost over. Funny thing, though. There seem to be all these pages tacked on here.

Alas. Didn't I tell you. Life is just one damned thing after another—no rest for the wicked. Or for the good either. This thought was borne in on me with particular poignancy one day last summer, when I was walking down Third Avenue with my teen-aged daughter. We were chatting idly, on our way to a movie. If you have adolescents, you know that moments like this are like the quiet passages in *Jaws*—precisely the time when you should be on guard, because that's when The Great White Shark is going to come thrashing into frame and bite off somebody's nose.

Anyway, she was in the midst of her first serious love affair, and so far as I could tell it was going along pretty well. But, out of nowhere, this dialogue arose:

"Dad, you've been around. Sort of."

"Yeah. Sort of."

"Well, er, you know I really like Stephen."

"So I gather."

"And mostly I like making out with him."

Stoic nod from Dad—no questions asked. I don't really

want to know just what "making out" entails among adolescents, circa 1980. I'm pretty sure, though, that things have changed since we were kids, when foreplay consisted of ten minutes of begging on my part, the upshot of which was usually an earnest discussion about whether or not I would "respect" someone who unlatched her bra before she was properly engaged.

"Well, um, what I wanted to ask was . . . ah . . . when you've been with someone for a while, do you, well, you know, get bored?"

"Kid," I said, "you've just asked the $64,000 question."

A little later a friend of mine who's in TV sent an associate off to cover an international conclave of sex therapists in Vienna or Budapest or some such spot, hoping a subject for a documentary program would present itself. Sure enough, on the last day of the conference, a panel of experts from around the globe were encouraged to expatiate on what each of them had found to be the most common presenting problem in their practices. No matter where they came from, or what kind of people they worked with, they all said the same thing. It was boredom.

And just the other day, thumbing through magazines on a drugstore rack, I found myself skimming an article in an eminently square and respectable woman's magazine in which six housewives engaged in a none-too-enlightening dialogue with a therapist about their common complaint—which was, you guessed it, bedroom boredom. On the same rack was another magazine carrying a piece on Walter Lippmann's love life, for God's sake. In it, the pundit of pundits was observed getting into trouble with a friend's wife because his marriage was—naturally—boring.

The point is obvious: whoever you are, wherever you go, no matter how much or how little experience you've had, eventually you—all of us—are going to encounter what I've come to think of as *the* problem, the thing that busts up—or anyway, bends—more marriages and more affairs than anything else.

For you, it is going to seem a particularly cruel issue. For the chances are that one of the things that went wrong with your marriage was that one—more likely, both—of you had become sexually stupefied about a decade or more of cohabitation, and in your innocence and isolation had imagined that the problem was singular to you, that no one else had ever endured that particular form of unpleasantness. And, indeed, in the first months of your new life as a single, it must surely have seemed that you were right, for you have experienced nothing like that old languidness of desire in the course of your several brief affairs. Quite the opposite, in fact.

Now, one of those sexually serendipitous adventures having gone marvelously in all other respects as well, you have decided to settle into some sort of mutually exclusive arrangement—if not living together right away, then seeing one another to the exclusion of all others. Whereupon, out of nowhere, there arises—to use exactly the wrong word—an old, familiar feeling: indifference. It strikes stealthily. One night she appears in the bedroom wearing her most demure nightie, plumps the pillows comfortably around her, and settles down with a big fat book she picked up on the way home. "I've just been dying for a good read," she says lightly. And at first you're relieved, as you scramble around on the night-table shelf, looking for last week's newsmagazine. "Been meaning to get to that cover story on the Joint Chiefs myself," you cheerily respond.

Next night, you decide to bring some reports home from your office. After all, you've been falling behind on that stuff ever since you took up with her. But from here on out, things deteriorate rapidly to the so-so level. The night you stay out later than you intended with Fred and Thelma—well, you *are* tired, you both agree. What's so terrible about getting a decent night's sleep for a change? Now it's Sunday morning. You've *always* stayed in bed, having your orange juice, reading the paper, fooling around. But the guys really can't seem to find a fourth for doubles, and all this soft living is taking its toll. It's really time you started getting back into shape again, isn't it?

By this time, of course, you're beginning to eye each other a little suspiciously. Does all this mean that the magic is draining out of your relationship? Is it becoming impossibly settled down, domesticated? So soon? And now the other gloomy musings come thicker and faster. That's it? These are the limits of her sexual inventiveness. And what about you? All those yummy fantasies you were one day going to act out with somebody you really cared about. How come they are but fading memories now? How come, if you want to know the truth, you're beginning to experience the odd—very odd, come to think of it—problem getting it up and keeping it there?

On top of which you have this bitter irony to contend with, namely, that you really like each other—you're easy and comfortable together, you laugh at the same jokes and like the same dishware. She does not put clown paintings on her bedroom wall and takes up tennis because she knows it will please you. For your part, you discover that you like the ballet almost as much as she said you would.

In short, here is the loveliness you always dreamed of, believed you were entitled to—that sweet sharing of lives that, long ago, when you were kids, you and your former wife thought you were creating. And might have, if all that child-rearing and career-making and general youthful stupidity hadn't intervened. Now, grown-up (more or less), you sense that life has given you a golden second chance at all that—that this, at last, is the lady you want, need, to make this mature effort with.

Except you're too tired at bedtime and too distracted in the daytime. And when you do actually join, there is something dutiful about the whole business. Naturally, the more the problem preys on your mind—and hers—the more awkward everything gets. One night somebody brings home *The Joy of Sex* (or gets it down from the highest shelf in the bookcase) and leaves it lying about casually. A little later she starts up about a weekend away again. And you both instinctively sense that this isn't going to be like that first weekend you finally agreed to a few months ago—was it really such a short time past?—that it has, implicitly, quite a different weight of meaning.

It may even work its brief magic. Lots of things—even, perhaps, *The Joys of Sex*—will have the same briefly arresting effect on your downward spiral. But it is humanly impossible to maintain, for any great length of time, the kind of sexual intensity that attends the mutual-discovery phase of a relationship. So around this time, one or the other of you is going to get worried enough about this matter to confide in a friend. And just as sure as you're born, he or she is going to reply to your earnest inquiry, "Well, Susan and I (or Al and I, whoever and I) had the same problem a few years back. And I'll tell you, we just decided that the only thing to do was to work at it."

Sounds good. After all, when everything else about a relationship is right, you will probably also be surprised to discover that it is not absolutely essential that it remain forever pitched at the fever levels of sexuality. In our time we have come to expect good sex—by which we actually mean the wildly passionate stuff that lifts us not only out of our socks, but out of our dailiness and out of ourselves—as a natural right. But I've looked, and nowhere do I find this particular privilege guaranteed us in the Constitution or the Bill of Rights. Once again, it's something the whole damned culture, from *Playboy* to the sex therapists, has conspired to sell us.

As a good relationship matures, other kinds of sexuality come into play. The affectionate kind, for instance. And the playful kind. And the kind that is more giving than receiving. And every once in a while—you'll see—the old-fashioned breathtaking kind pops up, too. Often when you least expect it.

What happens is that the overall mood of the relationship begins to condition the quality of its sexual expression (instead of the other way around). In other words, the earth doesn't have to move each and every time you touch. Sometimes it's good just to curl up in each other's arms and go to sleep, mutually trustful, mutually protective.

That is particularly true if you are enjoying "good communication" (groans from back of hall) on other levels. By which I mean you are talking. Women like to talk, men—especially American men—don't like to. It's what comes of seeing too many John Wayne movies at an impressionable age ("Never apologize, never explain; it's a sign of weakness"—*She Wore a Yellow Ribbon*). Anyway, once you're involved with a woman, you have got to stay in touch verbally. Now, at last, it's time to work on your parakeet imitation.

Here let me cite the evidence of that valuable witness to the life of our times, Ellen Goodman. She recently overheard, in a restaurant, that achingly familiar American female-male exchange in which she brightly inquires, "What are you thinking about?" and he replies, "Oh, nothing." What was sad about it to Ms. Goodman, and to me, was the fact that the coquettishly encouraging lady was in her eighties, and so was her verbally reluctant companion. They had obviously been playing and replaying this dumb scene for a half century.

"I have watched so many women leaning toward their men, as if their need pressed them into a dangerous incline," writes Ms. Goodman. "So many women asking for intimacy. So many women wondering, Is he thinking of her, of them." And, she adds, "I have seen so many men, too, removed or perhaps contained. So many men resisting this womanly intrusion into their privacy." She wonders, quite sensibly, if there isn't some double standard at work here, some perhaps genetically determined difference between the sexes regarding their needs in this matter.

But she rejects sexual determinism, and so do I. All that's happened, damn it, is that the traditional culture has done its work on us males, and it is essential, if we want to have and to hold a relationship, that we fight against all this strong, silent stuff. Silence is not, necessarily, a sign of strength. Very often it is a sign of stupidity. So speak up—prattle if you want to. In short, give. Or if you want a fancy literary reference, remember E. M. Forster's dictum: "Only connect."

You will recall the lady who referred me to the Bower Bird? Well, she threw another nice metaphor at me the other day— the rose and the stone. There are, she said, two kinds of relationships. There's the kind that's like a rose, which requires a great deal of delicate tending because you are conscious of its fragility and its mortality, but which is too beautiful, too poignant to be ignored. Then there's the other kind, which is like a stone. It is rough and simple and may have, if it's properly polished, a certain crude attraction, particularly since it requires almost no attention to survive. But, as she pointed out, we may perhaps place too much emphasis on guaranteed longevity. Her implication is that rose bushes are tougher than they look, have their interest in every season—even the fallow ones—and are capable of surprising adaptations, surprising new growths. And are, above all, living, changing, things. A stone, clearly, is not, and despite its deceptive solidity, can easily be stolen or just simply forgotten in its dullness and lack of color. And, of course, it rarely inspires poetry.

The thing to remember about a rose bush is that though it is always at risk, it is also entirely capable of lasting a lifetime, and beyond, if you nurture it lovingly. In the end, perhaps, you will transcend Masters and Johnson and, if you're lucky, the despairing impatience of your own restless impulses. Or, to put it simply, when boredom makes its inevitable appearance, try a little tenderness. Can't hurt, can it?

What to Do Until the Doctor Comes

But sex is no small thing. It's a basic thing. And once it goes stale and flat, I'm not at all certain there's a great deal that can be done about it. At this point, I'd like to call to the witness stand Mr. Woody Allen, who once said in an interview, "Each of us is so finely tuned that to have two people meet and intermesh is a matter of luck. I've had friends who when they marry say, 'I know we're going to have to work at it.' I always think they're wrong. The things that are really pleasurable in life, whether its playing softball or working on your stamp collection, really require no effort." I am not contradicting myself when I say that I think, by and large, he's right. Yes, you may want to apply some extra measures of common sense and uncommon sensitivity to the sexual issue, but if these fall over into the realm of highly conscious, if they become part of a Sisyphean burden instead of easing it, then, ladies and gentlemen, you'd better rethink the whole thing.

It is entirely possible, however, that if you are so devoted to the work ethic that you let it follow you into the bedroom, then these days it will occur to you that what's bothering you is not plain old-fashioned boredom, but real live "sexual dysfunction," as it's known in the trade. Whereupon one or the other of you will start thinking about the previously unthinkable—resort to a sex therapist. Now, it's perfectly true that a decade or so ago Masters and Johnson reported some startling results by having couples check into their institute in St. Louis, where, after appropriate examinations and counseling, they were set to rubbing one another with body oils in their motel rooms. At the time it seemed to me that almost anyone forced to hang around a motel room in St. Louis for a few days would sooner rather than later show more than usual interest in whoever he or she was sharing that experience with—body oils be damned. Some doubtless apocryphal explorer used to say that he knew it was time to leave the North Pole when the penguins started looking good to him.

And now the follow-up studies are beginning to support my cynicism. There are, it seems, a lot of shy, hung-up, and ill-educated people, people who require professional guidance (and reassurances) when it comes to exploring new positions, new orifices, new bedroom gadgetry, or, for that matter, buying a set of silk sheets for the bed. But, it seems, the effect of all these turn-ons is relatively short-lived, that they supply momentarily stimulating *frissons*—very nice and all—but cannot permanently reverse the course of boredom once it has started to run. You can probably obtain the same effects, at less cost, by simply letting your imagination run riot—or by taking Dr. Comfort seriously when you haul his tome down from the shelf. If not, well, it's your money and your ears that are going to be assaulted by therapeutic newspeak. Myself, I can't stand it.

What I can recommend—for a certain small percentage of the population, those who are not particularly afflicted by that curse of the modern age, a guilty conscience—is the discreet affair. I can just feel bristles rising all over the place. You're supposed to sort of slide into advice of that kind, but what the hell. Hear me out.

To begin with, "discreet" is the busily operative word in the foregoing. If bad sex is merely a metaphor for everything else that's wrong with the relationship, then I think it's more honest—and far less cruel—to deal openly with everything that's gone wrong, or bring the whole mistaken business to a quick and honest end. Do not start up an affair, however discreet you pretend you want to be, with the subconscious intention of its becoming visibly indiscreet in the end. Once, indeed, I indulged a lady in such an affair. That is to say, I was unattached at the time, and she was not, but professed herself restless, in need of some excitement on the sly. What she didn't tell me was that she was in the habit of keeping a diary, and that she sometimes sort of accidentally-on-purpose left it lying around where the guy she was living with could find it. I felt used, he felt abused, and a rather ugly telephonic scene ensued. There was, I'm certain, a better way for her, for anyone, to confront whatever was wrong in her life than to pull that particular stunt.

If, on the other hand, there is nothing much wrong with the rest of your relationship, then a quick fix of sexuality outside of it may be the very thing to quicken your pulse, freshen your fancies, and generally perk up the spirits—all of which may have a salutary effect on your basic relationship.

Please, no objections at this point. I've read the basic literature—*Madame Bovary* and *Anna Karenina* and all the other wonderfully romantic renderings of the perils of adultery—and, yes, I agree that we are trafficking here in adulterous emotions, even though the person you are cheating on is not your spouse in the eyes of the law. But these are new times, and it is completely possible to find members of the opposite sex who will understand your situation and not make a big fuss about it, who will not, for instance, start making strange phone calls at odd hours or dropping scented notes into the mail or generally make nuisances of themselves. The spirit is not quite zipless, but it is close enough. And it is sufficient unto your purposes.

The foregoing is, I admit, very cold-turkey. So I hasten to add that I don't think this sort of fooling around is for everybody. It is certainly not for the easily confused. By which I mean that if you're going to indulge in this sort of hanky-panky, you'd better be very clear going in that your aims are limited, and that you are not starting up a new hobby. You'd probably also be best off if you understood that the effect of an outside relationship on your basic relationship is likely to be temporary—like going to see the good doctors in St. Louis.

If, however, that's what you really want—and you find yourself wanting it repeatedly—face up to the essential faithlessness of your sexuality. Some people really are like that, and nothing is wrong with it, either, if you can stand the noise and the confusion—and act accordingly. In other words, don't go around seeking and promising faithfulness if you're not truly up to it. Which is, by the way, a judgment you shouldn't pass on yourself the first time a long-term affair goes wrong, but which after several such have gone awry sexually, is one you shouldn't hesitate to accept, either. It is *not written* that all of us will actually be happier living monogamously. For some, it is an unnatural act.

Just here, will you indulge me in one last bit of tough-mindedness? After almost five years of single life I have arrived at the most profound conviction that nothing in this life is permanent, although I am equally convinced that permanency is one of the several states of grace that some of us may accidentally arrive at. Or, to put the matter still more bluntly, it is not something that I think any of us—including the political conservatives and born-again religious—can either wish or will into existence by prating on about the sacredness of the family or the immutability of values that are essentially better suited to the more staid life of small agrarian communities in the pre-urban, pre-jet ages of the past. The anthropological and ethnological evidence continues to pile up—"Monogamy has never worked," as the anthropologist Robin Fox puts it. And many of us are bound to agree, not because we are smart-asses, but because we feel it in our rueful bones.

We are, therefore, conscious of the fact that we are ever at risk. Which means, to return to my basic point here, that it is always possible that if we are bored and restless in a relationship, our partner may very well be in the same state. And may, as quickly as we do, or more so, decide to do something about it. We know, as well, that when we indulge in something we fondly imagine to be nothing more than a palliative for our restlessness, the possibility always exists that it may turn into something more. That happy homes will, as a result, be broken up. That people will be hurt. That later we will be sorry for what we did. And wish that we could undo it.

"Left to their own devices," says our friend Fox, the anthropologist, "societies will work out some form of multiple mating system." Left to your own devices, so—frequently—will you. That, anyway, is my glum gloss on how the ape in us—formerly known, in less secular times, as the devil—will out. I neither condone nor condemn. I merely suggest that if pair-bonding (funny how infectious the vulgarisms of pseudo-science are) of a totally faithful kind turns out not to be your bag after you've given it a few tries, there's no point in feeling too guilty about it. There are, I assure you, women who share your lack of traditional moral fiber. And if you're willing to extend to one of them the same rights and privileges you insist on enjoying—some quiet slipping around—things will probably work out pretty well; you know, a few fights, a few sulks, the occasional dramatic carrying on, all of which will serve to remind you that you're both alive and kicking. Which is something else that some people need every now and then.

So much for the subversion of all our basic values. We may have, as Fox and his kind insist, an instinct for the polygynous, but we also have an impulse, I do believe, for peaceful cohabitation. We can't help but have it after a few centuries of propaganda in favor of it, and—after you've been divorced—a few months or years of a more harum-scarum sort of life. Frankly, I don't expect that you will be letter-perfect either in checking that instinct or in following that impulse—after all, the Pig Iron Convention *is* an annual event. But it should be possible, amongst civilized men and women to be faithful to the ideal of exclusivity while at the same time enjoying the occasional dip into fresh—and refreshing—waters. Did not F. Scott Fitzgerald suggest that the test of a good mind is the ability to entertain two seemingly contradictory ideas simultaneously? It should work out—if you keep your wits about you, bearing in mind that fun is fun and commitment is commitment, and that once you've made the latter, the former can be but a brief fling and a sometime thing.

Just Good Friends

Still and all... with the best of intentions... all those rationalizations... all that nurturing of the impulse to faithfulness ... the fact is that sometimes things just don't work out. As a matter of fact, most of the time—romantically speaking—things just don't work out. Always remember Woody's words: intermeshing is finally a matter of luck. And, as somebody else once said, "The heaviest object in the world is the body of the woman one has ceased to love."

These being the sad facts of life, you will soon enough discover that it requires just as much technique to get out of an affair as it does to get into one. And that this technique is much harder to come by, mostly because it's not something any sensible person wants to practice up on—it's like doing algebra in high school. Beyond that, of course, you are not practicing your wiles on some total stranger. This is a woman you once loved—maybe as recently as last Tuesday—someone who has shared her best and most intimate self with you, and vice versa, which means, if you have a shred of decency left in you, you don't want to play a lot of games with her after all this time. That's particularly true if you've been around a bit yourself and have had a few cute stunts pulled on you. Besides which, she knows all about you and your funny little ways. You aren't going to be able to charm your way out of this one.

It has been my experience that, for the most part, people do not end one relationship unless they have either begun another or are pretty certain they see a very lively possibility of one beginning—like tomorrow night. In other words, and no matter what they claim, people mostly do not break up a going thing, no matter how draggy it has become, unless they have an alternative in mind. Terrible, isn't it? How weak we are! How afraid we are of spending a few nights or—my God!—a few weeks by ourselves!

But this being the case, there are really no principles to invoke when the final crunch arrives. Probably one of two things has happened, and neither of them is really worth going into much detail about when you clear your throat and launch into what you imagine is going to be the final speech. (Though it probably won't be, life being the messy thing it is, so full of anticlimaxes.)

The first explanation is that you've been frightened off. It's all been so perfect that you don't see any honorable way out. What you're doing is facing up to the fact that you're not ready to commit to anyone on a permanent basis—not just yet. So, you start magnifying her little faults, until you've managed to talk yourself into believing that she's just not the right person for you. If you were honest with yourself you'd admit what you're doing, tell the lady that you've scared yourself witless, and see if she has any suggestions for cooling things out while you get hold of yourself. (Of course, if this particular headache persistently recurs in your life, you really ought to see your doctor.) But, naturally, you're not being honest with yourself—very few of us ever are in matters of this kind—and so what you've gone and done is allowed some little sideline flirtation or dalliance to get out of hand, and you are now convinced that you've found greener grass somewhere else. And you're feeling guilty about it. As well you should. Or you can no longer continue to make up lame excuses to both the ladies in question. Whatever.

Anyway, you're into it now, and the only question is what to say to the lady you're about to hurt. And goddammit, you'd better say something. The worst possible thing you can do is say nothing—just sort of disappear. You know how it is, you tell her you'll call tomorrow, and then, somehow, tomorrow you manage to get terribly busy, and then the next day you suddenly have to go out of town, and the day after that you promised to take the kids to the zoo, and ... And Saturday night is going to be the loneliest night in the week for her.

Besides you know, don't you, deep in your heart, that your little disappearing act is not going to work, that eventually she's going to swallow her pride and call you up, and that by this time her grievance is going to be doubled, for you have added a second dishonorability to your original crime of unfaithfulness. And that you don't need. At the very least, in an age when most of our relationships are, alas, both volatile and transitory, the basic thing we owe to one another is a set of good memories. No one is going to have good memories of a man last sighted skulking silently off into the shadows.

On the other hand, no one is going to have good memories of a man who handles a bust-up aggressively or accusatorily, either. There's been a great vogue in recent years for openness and honesty in our relationships, and I do agree that when a man and a woman make a serious, exclusive commitment to one another, they have to be able to discuss the little things that are bugging them, lest the small problems grow into big ones as they fester in the darkness.

But there is something terribly grim about all this à la mode forthrightness, and a degree of discretion seems to me a requisite in all of our dealings. Honesty, for all its virtues, is not a license to kill, and intimacy, among other things, provides us with information about our partner's worst fears and most profound insecurities. We all have something on those who are, or have been, near and dear to us—some weakness they have shame-facedly confessed to us, for example, or some behavioral mode that we have observed—which we need but to evoke in an argument in order to devastate them. You are not to do this. Ever. With anybody. No matter what the provocation. Because it's been done to you—probably as you and your former spouse were having at each other in the last exciting days of your marriage—and you know how it feels, which is rotten. Why would you now turn around and do the same thing to another human being, especially one who is more than likely nothing but an innocent party to your own craziness? And who, no matter what, has taken up no more than a few weeks or months of your life?

No, what you've got to do is face up honestly to whatever issues there are between you and the lady, lay them out as gently as possible, place most of the blame for this unhappy conclusion where it belongs—squarely on your own neurotic shoulders—and take the consequences. I think you should avoid, if you can, a long analytical wrangle, in which she attempts to point out to you—for your own future good—those sickly patterns she has observed in your way of life, of which this latest outrage is but the most self-destructive manifestation. You already know all this about yourself, for you've just rehearsed, in your own mind, the disheartening facts about your lacks and weaknesses in preparation for this encounter. She may need to get some of this out—as a face-saving device, and as a way of venting a lot of stuff she's been too decent to bring up while she still had some hopes for you. After all, fair's fair.

But a little of this material goes a long way, and at a certain point it's a good idea to agree with everything she's saying and end the discussion. Otherwise, you may find yourself replying by going into some of the ugly details of her inadequacies and thus violating the basic rule I laid down in the previous paragraph. The trick is to let her spit out her basic hurt and anger—you really do owe her that much—and then quickly and cleanly push off.

After you have pushed off, stay pushed off. Do not come paddling back to make what you insist—to yourself and to her—are innocent inquiries into the well-being of the jilted party. These can be misread as attempts to reopen. Come to think of it, that isn't a misreading at all. Nine out of ten times that's exactly what these sly little overtures are—even if you don't know or admit it. And they are probably not meant seriously. All you're really saying is that it's colder out there by yourself than you thought it might be. Or that the greener grass you thought you had spotted turned out to be, on closer inspection, Astro-turf.

Well, tough. The most basic thing I've learned about the single life, the most morally salutary thing about its many ups and downs, smiles and frowns, is that they finally teach you, so you know it in your bones, the most fundamental tenet of existential philosophy, namely that *you must live with the consequences of your actions.*

This is a truth that is difficult enough to grasp in the best of times, and these are not the best of times for getting hold of it. Corporations, governments—all of our most basic institutions—offer, among other delights, the opportunity to fudge on this point. For they are all, at bottom, committees, and we all know that the function of a committee is to spread the responsibility for any action (and, of course, to blunt the thrust of that action, by softening and compromising it right from the start) and then to make sure that the blame for it, when it goes wrong, is apportioned among many hands.

Well, you're on your own now, making your own mistakes. And, when you end a relationship—or take up a new one—

you cannot foresee the consequences of that action. If, however, you take it, you must be prepared for the unexpected, for the possibility that time will show you that you've made not merely a forgettable little mistake, but a great walloping one. And you are going to make a bunch of them—that much, at least, you can count on. But there is no one you can go whimpering to—except, of course, yourself.

The only consolation I can offer is that, in time, you will toughen up without, I hope, becoming cynical. By which I mean that you will learn a certain stoicism, an acceptance of the fact that life is full of possibilities for awful errors and that you surely do commit your fair share of them. This will have the effect, ultimately, of making you more tolerant of other people's blunders, perhaps more acceptant of the fact that, over the long haul, you will yourself be victimized about as often as you victimize in matters of the heart. Another way of putting it is that there is no hope for immediate, eye-for-eye justice when a pair splits, and one party bears more of the hurt than the other. But a rough justice does pertain over the long run: overall, you can count on getting screwed about as often as you get to do the screwing.

Finally, the New Celibacy

I always keep my promises. Somewhere, a few dozen pages back, I told you that there would come a time when you would really need a little time to yourself. Well, this is it—when a really serious affair breaks up, one in which you both had a lot at stake. Hard enough to give up the pleasant customs you evolved together; even worse to abandon the future that you just couldn't help starting to imagine together. It seemed so real. And now it's all gone. My God, you spent so much time together that you don't even have a love letter to moon over— just that little pile of shells you collected that time at the beach, and they look awfully white and dry.

This may or may not be the worst loss you've suffered in a long time, but however you rank it, a loss it surely is. So mourn. Decently. Without too much drama. Or self-indulgence. And keep to yourself for a while. You're not going to cut much of a romantic figure anyway for a few weeks.

This may seem to contradict my earlier advice about going right back into the air after a crash, but I don't think so. By this time you will have earned your wings many times over— you don't have to prove anything to anybody, least of all yourself. Thus there will come a time when your need not to hear the motors roaring all the time will not be quite so desperate. And this ought to be that time.

It is all right, at this point, to take some time off in a quiet region of your own devising. One of the nice things about being single is how, if you're active enough, television has ceased to be a factor in your life. Well, now is your chance to check back in and see how, if anything, TV has become more rotten than ever. Also, when they come up in conversation, you will at last be able to put a face to those mysterious names—Erik Estrada, Priscilla Presley—you've been hearing about. Or you can catch up on some reading. Or write a few letters. Or see some of the guys. Or just take a beat and think about where you've been and where you might like to go next.

One of the places you might like to go is back to one of the ladies you once loved. I know, I know—it sounds crazy after everything that I said in the previous chapter. But that was really the point of it. If you made your exit with at least minimal grace, and if you've allowed a few healing months to pass, and if she's somebody you had good, basic communication with, then it should be possible to reconstitute the relationship.

On an entirely new basis, of course, because we're still talking celibacy here. If you start thinking about going back just because you're lonesome and you'd like a quick, nostalgic roll in the hay, forget it. But if you weren't an absolute plonk, and she wasn't, then it's just possible that you can go back as a friend and even, perhaps, a confidant. After all, you know each other pretty damn well, and if you've got some troubles she may have some pretty shrewd advice to offer now that your passions have cooled. Of course, this has to be a tit-for-tat arrangement. You've got to be willing to hear her out on whatever is bugging her at the moment.

But just as it is absolutely essential for a single man to

have disinterested—but not uninterested—female friends to consult on certain delicate matters, so does the single woman require men friends to give her the male slant on things. Since one of the few measurable—and unquestionably valuable—bits of progress we've made in recent years lies in the fact that it is now possible for men and women to be "just good friends" and mean it, you would be foolish not to take advantage of this precious situation. And to do so with a lady on whom you can't pull any of your usual fast shuffles. Also, you will find it handy—just as she will—to have some neutral but friendly party you can invite to be your escort on those social occasions when you just can't deal with the occasion and a strange date simultaneously. Naturally, not all of your old flames are going to take kindly to proposals of friendship (By the same token, there are going to be a number of old flames that *you're* going to find excuses not to meet when they call up to suggest having a drink.) But if you let enough time pass, and if your heart is really pure, then you ought to be in a position where, though you may have many ex-lovers, you have almost as many new friends. As I say, modern life is full of many surprising turns. Not all of which are unpleasant.

Into the Valley of the Wimps

Great advice, Dick! Just terrific! What a wonderful life you must have led!

Well, er, um. See, here's the thing ...

Let me put that another way. A certain amount of what I've had to say so far is based on hindsight—the kind of good ideas we all tend to have about half an hour after they should have occurred to us, when we're walking down the street muttering to ourselves.

Now I don't mean to imply that I haven't managed to end some affairs neatly, with no hard feelings and a firm friendship the final result. Or that certain ladies have not managed the same trick with me. But it is only fair to say that these have been affairs between two people who could plead temporary sanity before, during, and after the event. There are, for instance, affairs of another sort, affairs that leap up out of nowhere, burn with searing intensity for a relatively brief time, and then simply die, consumed in their own heat. You aren't going to emerge from those unscathed. And neither party is going to feel much like being old buddies afterward, mostly because friendship, in the conventional sense, was never part of the highly combustible mixture that spontaneously ignited in the first place.

But there is at least one advantage to these wildfires of unknown origin: they burn so fast and clean that they tend to leave no nasty residue, no ashy regrets to pick through, looking for clues as to what went wrong, what you should do differently in the future. For there's nothing to be learned about this kind of thing, except to enjoy the thrill of it while it lasts—because it isn't gonna last long. All you can say is that every boy (and every girl) should have one or two such experiences in this life, just to see that life, besides imitating Theodore Dreiser, can also imitate trashy, hard-breathing, page-turning novels that are beneath literary contempt but nevertheless provide all of us—no matter how grand our pretenses—with a bracing dose of guilty pleasure now and then.

There is another sort of inexplicable affair that *is* going to leave you feeling pleasurelessly guilty—guilty about your own stupidity, that is—and which contains very little that is agreeable while it is proceeding and even less in reminiscence. There is no convenient name for this kind of thing, and not much you can do to avoid it, I do believe. But forewarned is about as forearmed as you can get, and I would be remiss in my duties if I did not discuss it at some length, for in the lists of love, this is the killer. And the one upon which you should use your new-found skill at endings almost immediately—like after your first date.

You usually meet your fatal femme when you least expect to and, if I may say so, when you least deserve to. That is to say, the months have passed, you have gained from the range of your romantic experiences a sense that there's nothing you can't handle—be it a one-night stand, or a live-in arrangement—with a certain amount of style and grace. And, of course, you have acquired all the evidence any reasonable human being could require that you are an attractive, viable chap, no matter what your ex-wife thinks. In short, you have survived, and damned if it doesn't look as if you're going to endure.

Except. Except that despite all the fun and frolic your new life has provided, all the chills and spills and moments of startling, breathtaking warmth that you never thought you'd experience again in this life, the fact remains that it also has its emptinesses, based on the growing suspicion that maybe all your recent activity has less to do with loving than it does with scoring, that it is time at last to settle down seriously to the business of settling down. A perfectly reasonable thought. But, watch it. For survival has brought you to an unsuspected moment of arrival—at your moment of maximum danger. It is just now that you are your most overconfident and, therefore, most vulnerable state. And so it will be that you meet her, the one who will administer your final, most devastating instruction in the ways of a maid with a man.

In my case, she was a small, dark lady with large brown eyes, in which I so quickly lost myself that I never noticed in them the glint of hard calculation and total self-absorption. What I did notice was that she had all sorts of vitality, an interesting career, and everything that I cared about she also seemed to care about. Why, we even came from similar backgrounds. And we were always terrific together in bed. Best of all, the timing seemed right. I was looking to settle down, and she was coming out of a long, unsatisfying affair, she said.

At first, things progressed in a sensible and gratifying way—initial wariness giving way to growing affection, which was, in turn, replaced by what seemed to be a glowing passion. She lived in Los Angeles but came to New York for four days on her way to London for a Christmas holiday. We took my children ice-skating. She met my friends. I met her friends. We made love at all times of the day and night. We could not stop touching each other. We could not go to sleep because there was so much to talk about. On the afternoon she was to leave, I made one of my grand and glamorous gestures; I bought a ticket for London, threw some clothes in a bag, and got on the plane with her. That gray and glorious city fashioned a wreath of carols around us, and we—or was it only I?—moved through its shops and theaters and restaurants under a spell of romantic enchantment.

And then the week ended, with presents and promises on Christmas morning, and our separate airplanes bore us off in separate directions, and when we met, a couple of weeks later, we were suddenly three. *He*—whom I had been helping her get over—had suddenly returned to her life, full of apologies and threats and reformations. I did the manly thing: choose, I said, choose between the known past (dismal him) and the unknowable future (interesting me, loving us).

Well, she chose—without choosing. That is to say, she requested time to work things out. He was such a troubled guy. And also he was a type you often encounter in these situations—a terrorist. He would threaten harm to himself; he was a master of the three a.m. phone call and the equally well-timed ring on the doorbell. In short, he was such a total asshole that I decided to hang around, figuring it was only a matter of time before he simply destroyed himself in her eyes.

Do not ever figure that way. It is the first step down the road to wimpdom. If she will not choose you—clearly, cleanly, and early—then follow that first impulse: walk and keep walking, without looking back. She might just follow, but the thing is eventually you're going to have to take that walk anyway, and the longer you wait, the more crippled your stride will become. By the time I finally took off (more months later than I'm going to admit publicly), I was on my hands and knees.

For she turned out to be, as her type always tends to be, tough, manipulative, emotionally impoverished, entirely selfish—and all the time butter wouldn't melt in her mouth. If you want a literary reference, you might care to check out F. Scott Fitzgerald's lovely short story "Winter Dreams," in which he described the type and the way she operates with what seems to me immortal perfection: "She had treated him with interest, with encouragement, with malice, with indifference, with contempt. She had inflicted on him the innumerable little slights and indignities possible in such a case—as if in revenge for having ever cared for him at all. She had beckoned him and yawned at him and beckoned him again and he had responded often with bitterness and narrowed eyes. She had brought him ecstatic happiness and intolerable agony of spirit. She had caused him untold inconvenience and not a little trouble. She had insulted him and ridden over him, and she had played his interest in her against his interest in his work—for fun. She had done everything to him except to criticize him—this she had not done it seemed to him because it might have sullied the utter indifference she manifested and sincerely felt toward him."

The only difference between my case and the one Fitzgerald wrote up for the annals was that his antiheroine, Judy Jones by name, drove her guy crazy with many men; mine had only the one. And what she was doing was not so much setting me up as a fall guy but as a fall back—in case her other turkey started to roost elsewhere again. She did, however, keep offering false hope that someday she would free herself of him. On those occasions when I made my abortive little flights for freedom, she would always welcome me back and sometimes even find ways to pull me back. Beyond that, through thin and thin, the sex stayed marvelous, perhaps because in part she dared not ever speak to him about me, despite the fact that I knew all his comings and goings—"I can't say anything; he's so much crazier than you are"—though by this time neither of us would have been chosen as the poster boy for mental health week. I mean, maybe it was precisely the air of illicitness that his lurking presence lent to our affair that kept it sexually fresh.

But look, credit where credit is due. Whatever quiet lunacy she was operating out of (and I suspect that, in part, she was but doing unto me precisely what the other guy was doing unto her—jerking me around out of some awful desire to control and maneuver another human being for the sickly fun of it), the fact remains that *I let her do it*. For whatever their illusions and delusions, our tormentors in these situations could not impose them on the rest of us if we were not the prisoners of our own sad muddles. In the end, in matters of this kind the only delusions that count—that can really move us—are self-delusions. You enter the Valley of the Wimps under your own steam, propelled by your own demons. No one—except myself, of course—made me grateful to accept those Tuesday-night dates when he got Fridays and Saturdays. And that was me agreeing to let her leave my bed at midnight or one a.m. so she would be at home to accept his calls when he was out of town. And it was the same fellow agreeing never, never to call her when he was in town, then waiting around the house hoping every time the phone rang it would be her (only it never was). Yes, naturally, a woman creates desire in one, but only fools like me can make an obsession. And you, brother.

A psychiatrist named Robert J. Stoller recently hypothesized that sexual excitement of the kind that can turn you into a wimp is based on hostility, the absence of which "leads to sexual indifference and boredom." On the other hand, he says, the hostility implicit in a highly erotic relationship "is an attempt, repeated over and over again, to undo childhood traumas and frustrations that threatened the development of one's masculinity or femininity." Talk about your Catch-22s! But, by golly, I think he's got hold of something there, because I did have the feeling when I was caught up in my obsession that I was trying to finish, with this lady, some half-forgotten, but unsatisfactorily abandoned, conversation of the past. And I had the feeling that she was often engaging in a similar effort.

It may be, *pace* Stoller, that that unfinished conversation was with ourselves. Somebody, I think it was Jung, said that obsession occurs when we find someone who, all unawares, completes something that only our unconscious senses is missing in ourselves. I still don't know what was incomplete in me. Maybe it was that she had been a Kappa in college and I'd never had much luck with them. What I do know is that, in its early stages, wimpish obsession very closely resembles the stuff of popular romantic fictions of the kind M-G-M used to feed us—the mother's milk of the damaged middle-aging psyche. You remember those movies: for seven reels the girl carries on with Mr. Wrongo while the Jimmy Stewart type moonily hangs around, his Adam's apple bobbing up and down in silent romantic agitation, and in the eighth reel she notices him and his faithfulness is rewarded. Well, gentlemen, that was just a movie, not life. In life, the Jimmy Stewart type gets to pick her up after her exercise class and to spend a lot of time at home thumbing through *Playboy*, claiming he buys it for the interview.

In my heart of hearts I don't believe there's anything to be done about the Valley of the Wimps. The TVA is not going to buy it, flood it, and make it part of a new hydroelectric project. Or, to change the metaphor, and to quote a wise older friend of mine, whose eyes were politely crossing as one of my recitals of pain entered its second hour one lunchtime: "My boy, you're going to have to walk this road to the end." He was right; there's no shortcut out of the valley. Moreover, it constitutes a dark passage that every man (and most women, too), regardless of age, marital status, or station in life must endure once in his life—unless you married your high school sweetheart and have remained entirely faithful ever since. I know—a year ago I did a lot of asking around. (That was about the time this terrible rash broke out on my hands and the dermatologist asked me if I'd been under any strain lately.) Everybody's gone through it. Or will go through it. But on the off chance that we can learn anything worthwhile from someone else's experience, I have compiled a little quiz for would-be lovers. If you are in the midst of what you fondly believe to be a genuine love affair, and if you answer "yes" to more than one of these questions, recognize that the movie you're playing in is not some elegant Lubitsch romance but *Of Human Bondage*, being remade one more dismal time.

THE WIMP QUIZ

1. Are you afraid to run out and pick up your shirts at the Chinese laundry because you're sure that's when she'll finally make the phone call she promised you?
2. Do you plan your route to and from work so that it takes you by her house, hoping that your passing will coincide with the time she walks her dog?
3. Does an enervating sentimentality come over you when you happen to walk by that little French restaurant where she laughed immoderately at your jokes; the street corner where she was actually on time for a date; the movie theater where the revival of *Beat the Devil* turned out to be as funny as you promised her it would be?
4. Do you find yourself talking obsessively about her to friends despite their desperate efforts to change the subject?
5. Do you have a drawerful of letters to her—angry, cajoling, passionate, mature, and wise (often within

the same paragraph) in their observations about her potential and that of your partnership—which you've never dared mail?

6. Will you pick up her prescription for her—her tomatoes?—even though the store really isn't on the way to her house?
7. Do you quietly leave the room when you're visiting and *he* calls? Even when it's the second time in the same evening? The third?

And so forth. As I say, there is no cure for this nonsense. Except not to let it get started in the first place, to which end you are invited to clip out my little quiz and keep it handy so you can refer to it at the first sign of a sniffle. Once the disease has taken hold, all you can do is surrender to it, as with flu, and let it run its course.

But enough. No more cute stuff. We're not talking flus and viruses and other quotidian nuisances. We're talking about something that is, in many cases, much more serious. What we're talking about, by God, is obsession.

We are also talking about something that can get you in trouble with the law. No kidding. What happens is that in the depths of your hopelessness and craziness, you start mailing those letters to her in which you analyze her problems for her—for her own good, naturally, you old altruist you. Or you take to hanging around on the street outside her apartment and accosting her when she goes out for the groceries. One friend of mine found himself summoned to the lady's lawyer, who threatened to have him up on charges if he didn't stop those calls and letters. Another acquaintance actually opened his door one morning to find a man from the D.A.s office standing there with a summons. There are, actually, laws against harassment, which is what persistent intrusion on someone's privacy in order to tell them things they don't want to hear amounts to.

But let's imagine you manage to stay out of the cops' clutches. You're still a pretty sick kid. A witty friend of mine, who happens to be a horsewoman, says that when she sees a full-blown case of it, she is reminded not of any human disease, but of something called The Wobbles, which afflicts horses and cows. What happens when they come down with it is that they walk around and around in circles. Until they drop. Dead.

That's pretty good, and you're welcome to that description if you like. Myself, I prefer something a little more vividly disgusting. I've come to think of obsession as the tapeworm of the soul. Something mindlessly insatiable gnawing away at you in the dark. And a killer if you ignore it, just sort of hope it'll go away.

...And Out of It

As I say, there isn't much you can do about wimpishness once you are caught in its thrall (though I think calling what ails you by its rightful name—not pretending that you are some kind of great romantic hero—does help). The irony is that it is only she, the one who enthralled you, can finally set you free, which she will accomplish in the same way that she accomplished your enslavement—without knowing what's she's doing.

Here's what will happen: Like any master, she gets used to having her servant hanging around, unquestioning, doing what he's told. Then one day she will pull one of her usual stunts—"Gosh, I know I said we could spend this weekend together, but now Steve's decided he wants me to come with him to that party after all; but listen, I've got *all* afternoon free on Sunday"—and that, especially if you've somehow finally gotten it straight in your mind that this can't be love because you feel so bad, will be that. The clanging sound you hear will be the scales falling from your eyes and landing down around your ankles. Uttering the greatest wimp exit line of all time—"Frankly, my dear, I don't give a damn"—is purely optional.

What's ludicrous is how small the affront that finally

brings a grand lunatic passion to an end usually is—I keep telling you, life is not a movie—and how amazingly soon the scars heal. Curiously, you'll find after a bit that you don't even regret the time so fecklessly spent. Because it wasn't wasted. Just the opposite, I think, for the function of these wretchedly flawed, inevitably failed, relationships is to complete your sentimental education.

To begin with, you should learn from an affair of this order that there are, in this world, women who simply have no talent for loving. By this I mean simply that they are infected with a terrible emotional caution, a bone-deep sense that love must inevitably diminish rather than enhance them. They know, naturally—frequently they blame it all on their daddies, who yelled at them a lot—that this is an unhealthy state, and they really try to break out of it, which is why the first few weeks with them always go so nicely. It is always at the point where the obstacles should start tumbling down that they start building them up. There is always a career, a married man, or an emotional cripple lurking in the shadows of their lives, ready to be summoned forth to provide the previous commitment that is no commitment, so she can avoid the real thing and thus avoid spoiling the perfection of her self-absorption. Diane Keaton gave us a letter-perfect interpretation of the type in *Manhattan,* and Woody Allen uttered the line that summarized everything you need to know about her: "You always think you'll be the one to change her—but you never are." Well, now you've learned the hard way how right he is. So you'll never have to go through all that again, will you?

You will also have learned, I hope, that if there are these women who lack a talent for loving, it stands to reason that there are an equal number of men of similar character around and about, and that it is entirely possible that you may be one of them. I'm not saying that you definitely are, but if you have all along been looking for relationships that aren't really relationships, that provide safe havens for your free-floating romantic fancies, because you know—or sense—that in one of them you can protest your passion as noisily as you want in complete security that it will not really be reciprocated, then you may be in trouble, having the fun of acting like you're in love without ever having to make a genuine commitment.

Recently a psychologist named Dorothy Tennov invented a term for and wrote a book about people who are devoted to being in this condition, which she called "limerence." Put simply, what these people love is the state of being in love, not of loving. Byron, she surmised, was such a person; so were a lot of historical characters we like to regard as great romantics. And maybe they were, in a sense, for is it not the essence of the great romantic tales that they must end tragically, with some insuperable difficulty preventing a permanent liaison from being consummated? Nowadays, of course, there are no such difficulties. Class distinctions are no longer rigidly enforced, moral and religious principles are honored only on state occasions, distance is diminished by jet planes and long-distance telephones, and so our modern-day Tristans and Isoldes, our Abelards and Eloises, do not end up dead as a result of their romantic transgressions, but with a mild hangover caused by overindulgence in that new food of the gods, "guilt"—a condition that can be cured by popping two psychological aspirins at your next appointment with the shrink.

All of this being the general case, isn't it nice that we have limerence to fall back on, that we can carry in our own minds, some of us, the necessary bars to commitment and permanency? In the aftermath of an affair with someone of this character, it seems to me a very good idea to examine your own motives in allowing yourself to fall under someone's thrall, to see if, perhaps, this woman did not serve some unacknowledged need for limerence on your part. It's also not a bad idea to examine your own past behavior—and future intentions—to see if you have not, yourself, caused misery of the kind you have just suffered. For it seems logical to me to suppose that if one's desire is merely to busy oneself inconclusively with an affair, to enjoy the storms and strifes of love without its longer-lasting consequences, then it can make little difference whether one plays the role of victim or victimizer. The end result is the same.

And another thing. The wimpish affair should cause you to reflect on a simple fact: all love relationships, no matter how principled they may seem, are also, inevitably, power relationships. It is very rare for both parties to love each other to precisely the same degree. One is bound to be slightly more in love or more needful or more vulnerable than the other. And that grants to the one who is less enamored—even if only by a little bit—the power position. He or she can always walk away less painfully than the other. That should impose on that person a sense of responsibility; in extreme cases not to play the sadist to the other's masochist, and in the more usual circumstances, to end the affair quickly and cleanly when you become aware of your true feelings, or rather lack of same. In other words, wimpishness is unisex, so the rule is: "Neither a wimp nor a wimp-maker be." For heaven's sake, remember what it feels like, and be kind.

Self-knowledge, then, is one of the consolations that makes traversal of the Valley of the Wimps an experience not totally without value, and that new awareness of self should certainly include a newly quickened sense of just how deep is your own downside—the indignities you are, I hope, utterly amazed to discover you are capable of forcing upon yourself. I think, perhaps, we must all journey once through the Valley in order to see, in yet another light, just how fragile we are— and how powerful our sense of survival can be once we discover how threatened we can be by what started out looking like love.

There are even, I've discovered, some more positive lessons to be learned from this experience. I owe to Richard C. Wedemeyer, of Athens, Georgia, the best of the expressions I have heard on this point. He was one of many readers who responded thoughtfully, and with great openness, to the original version of this book when it appeared in *Esquire*. He said, in part, "There is a fine difference between a wimp and a loving, caring person. The line is impossible to define, and it really serves no purpose to try. The deeply sensitive and non-ego-oriented man is the one who may readily become a wimp . . . the less emotional, less chance-taking man can claim he is never a wimp. But who is better off?"

Who, indeed? Looked at after the experience has been fully digested, one can see that, revising a familiar phrase, everything has been lost save honor. And that, therefore, nothing has been lost. For if you have conducted yourself with full heart and full energy, you will have discovered that you are capable of emotions that you probably didn't know you possessed, that, of all things, the loser in the situation is not you but the other, for to be the recipient of the kind of passion you generated could have been transforming—if only she had let it be. And anyway, aside from looking a little bit foolish—wasn't the first time, won't be the last—you probably have not done yourself any permanent damage. Indeed, you may possibly have gained a pearl that is without price, namely, the capacity to recognize true love when you finally find it. And very simple it is to identify: it's the exact opposite of what you've just gone through.

A Final Confession

It took me a very long time to write the magazine article from which this book stems—writing personally always does. And in the course of that time, of all things, I managed to fall in love. Anything for a big finish, right?

Wrong. I wasn't expecting to fall in love. Didn't particularly want to. Not right now, anyway. Besides, she's an actress—a breed I warned you about at the beginning of this book. But she is also a woman of mature accomplishment in many other respects as well, one who gives a first and quite correct impression of great self-possession—warm and interested, yet also polite and distant. She keeps very much to herself, despite a life that has been lived mostly in the public eye. But there was something about her ... some knowing humor in her eyes, some blend of compassion and curiosity and just plain decency that I sensed and which compelled me to try to get to know her better, and not necessarily in the Biblical sense of the term. And so, not greatly encouraged by her, I pursued her, by letter and long-distance and finally by jet, to that quiet and faraway place where, periodically, she retreats from the world.

There, to put the matter with the discretion she so highly values, our affair prospered. Why, a full moon lit our path up the glen to the place where the waterfall begins its rush into the stream below. The months have gone by, and still we prosper. Our love is, I suppose, like all other loves in its broadest aspects, but it is singular in small ways that I will not describe, simply because they belong to us and to no one else. I will content myself merely by saying that she is the most generous human being I have ever known, and that she has taught me something of what it is like not to count costs or consequences. She also combines, with her wisdom, a sweet innocence—and a capacity to laugh at it—that is not only endearing but instructional. I think I'm beginning to lose some of the worldliness that has encrusted me, without my being entirely aware of it, over the years. She has taught me, also, the value of separation, for she must, sometimes, be alone, away from the world, away even from those who love her.

I do not especially like that, but I have ceased to think of it as a "problem." We all have our necessities, and they must be respected. I have some of my own—places I must go, things I must do, responsibilities I can't shirk—and she permits me these without complaint. It has become part of our way of being. And when we are apart on our separate errands, we are armored by our knowledge that what we have had is safe, beyond hurt in memory, while what we may have yet together is fragile, entirely susceptible to the dangers of carelessness and indifference, and, therefore, to be cared for by the best spirits that we can summon up from within us. There is no anxiety in this, no desperation—only a sort of tender patience. We have already had, I think, more than I ever dared hope for, and so, humanly, I want more—as much more as I am to be allowed. I pray she feels the same. I hope good luck attends us. But if it were all to end tomorrow, then there would be sadness but no regrets, for we already possess a deeply shared past, precious and incommunicable to others.

When we are apart, we busy ourselves productively, but

each day there comes a moment when the time hangs heavily, and my thoughts turn inevitably to her. In memory, in those moments, she is lit always by the glow of candles and of hearth, which is appropriate, I think, to a woman who seems to have been delivered into my arms via time warp, a creature out of some romantic fiction, spunky and independent, no nonsense about her. Except, you will recall, those fine-spirited ladies were always tremulous romantics at heart, and always possessed of the gift of giving.

In these moments of reflection, I know that without the clumsiness, stupidity, and pain of the passages I've been describing herein, I would not have known enough, a year ago, to recognize and reach out toward her singularity. Nor would I have possessed the cunning to pursue her—if I say so myself—as artfully as I did. Nor the determination I feel to see through with her whatever perils the unknown future holds, to grasp as long as I am able, this happiness, this contentment. Nor, finally, the simple common sense, bred of experience, to appreciate what I have found in her, and through her, in me. I find, not to put too fine a point on it, that I am able to trust again—not just her but myself, which, as it happens, is the hardest thing for me. We give to each other and receive from each other, and in these acts of loving-kindness there is gaiety and gravity and a special grace that fills up, at last, the wondering heart.